CW00371471

Challenging Local Authority Decisions

Ann McDonald

VENTURE PRESS

© Ann McDonald, 1997

All rights reserved. No part of this publication may be reproduced, stored in a retrieval system, or transmitted, in any form or by any means, electronic, mechanical, photocopying, recording or otherwise, without the prior permission of Venture Press

Published by
VENTURE PRESS
16 Kent Street
Birmingham
B5 6RD

British Library Cataloguing-in-Publication Data
A catalogue record for this book is available from the British Library

ISBN 1-86178-015-X (paperback)

Design, layout and production by
Hucksters Advertising & Publishing Consultants,
Riseden, Tidebrook, Wadhurst, East Sussex TN5 6PA

Cover design by:
Western Arts
194 Goswell Road
London
EC1V 7DT

Printed in Great Britain

Contents

Dedication
To Felicity, with love.

Acknowledgements
I would like to acknowledge, with thanks, the encouragement and help of the following people: Colleagues in the School of Social Work of the University of East Anglia; Margaret Taylor, solicitor and partner in the firm of Ward Gethin (Kings Lynn); and Georgina Henry-Routledge.

Introduction

Local authority decision-making is founded on a mixture of statutory powers and duties, regulations, and directions and guidance from central government. There is nevertheless scope for considerable discretion within this statutory brief. How it is interpreted will vary from authority to authority, but it will always operate within a framework of political accountability (to the Social Services Committee); resource availability, both financial and otherwise; and the skills and values of individual decision-makers. Part of this essential knowledge is an awareness of the range of challenges possible against local authority decisions which do not appear to correspond to the duties and powers imposed on local authorities by the legal structure, or which are contrary to the principles of good administration. An absence or misuse of proper channels for the redress of grievances disempowers service users and undermines the integrity of professional workers who seek to follow good practice. Though this book concentrates specifically on challenging local authority decisions within the fields of child care and community care, much of what is said is relevant to other decision-making bodies in other fields.

THE LEGISLATIVE FRAMEWORK

The Children Act 1989 and the National Health Service and Community Care Act 1990 together provide the broad framework within which decision-making takes place. The genesis of the two Acts was very different. The Children Act 1989 was based on a legal and professional consensus that the existing law was muddled and needed fundamentally to be reframed into a single code which would reflect the paramountcy of the welfare of the child and the need to work in partnership with parents. The National Health Service and Community Care Act 1990 by contrast is a minimalist piece of legislation which creates a new duty upon local authorities to assess the need for community care services, but which refers back entirely to previous legislation to define what those services should be. It contains no value statement, and was not professionally driven, but was based on the ideology of consumerism and competition, evidenced through the creation of a purchaser provider split. There are however similarities between the Children Act 1989 and the National Health Service and Community Care Act 1990 which make comparison worthwhile: both contain the notion of assessment of need as a gateway to services; both are based to varying degrees on the assumption that a mixed economy of care between the public and independent sectors is to be encouraged; and both contain quality assurance mechanisms (such as reviews) and their own (separate) complaints procedures. Though the subject matter with which they deal is very different, the sort of issues that they throw up for consideration will be similar.

THE STATUS OF GUIDANCE

Much modern day legislation is no more than broad statements of principle, the meaning of which is fleshed out by later regulations, guidance documents and practice guides. Legislation subsequent to the National Health Service and Community Care Act 1990; namely the Carers (Recognition and Services) Act 1995 and the Direct Payments Act 1996 are good examples of this sort of legislation, quickly put together to fill a legislative vacuum. Ironically, such widely drafted legislation creates more opportunities for challenge, particularly legal challenges because no-one is quite sure what the legislators intended to mean by a particular word or phrase. The proper construction of statutes is the task of the courts, and it is their prerogative to disagree with the interpretation put on the statute by the Minister in subsequent guidance if they see fit.

The distinction between regulations, directions and guidance is well described in the Introduction to 'The Care of Children: Principles and Practice in Regulations and Guidance' (HMSO, 1989). First in the hierarchy come regulations which, provided they are properly made under a power conferred by the parent Act, are subordinate legislation, and as such have the full force of a statute. The Boarding Out Regulations are an example of the use of this power, as are the Residential Care Homes Regulations made under the authority of the Registered Homes Act 1984. Guidance documents are usually issued as Circulars by the Secretary of State for Health, and if appropriate, they may be copied as guidance for health authorities as 'Health Service Guidance'. Thus the Circular on continuing care, which for local authorities is LAC(95)5 is for Health Authorities HSG (95)8. Formal guidance (or 'policy guidance') will specifically state that it is issued under the authority of s.7(1) of the Local Authority Social Services Act 1970. Section 7(1) says that

> *'Local authorities shall, in the exercise of their social services functions, including the exercise of any discretion conferred by any relevant enactment, act under the general guidance of the Secretary of State.'*

This means that there is a presumption that local authorities will have regard to such guidance. All of the volumes of guidance issued under the Children Act 1989 have the status of s.7(1) guidance. The Policy Guidance 'Community Care in the Next Decade and Beyond' (1990) is also s.7(1) guidance. Failure to take such guidance into account will be good grounds for challenging decisions made in disregard of it. This does not mean that guidance can never be departed from; what it does mean is that acting differently should be a considered and justifiable decision. This was the view taken of the Policy Guidance by Sedley J. in *R. v. Islington London Borough Council, ex parte Rixon* The Times, April, 17, 1996 when considering its relevance to the assessment and care planning process. The implication is that both local authority policies and procedures, and individual care planning decisions should explicitly be based on a sound understanding of the guidance. Section 7A(1) of the Local Authority Social Services Act 1970 also enables the Secretary of State to issue Directions to local authorities. The difference is that whilst local authorities must act 'under' guidance (with some scope for deviation) they must act in accordance with directions and have no choice but to follow them. Directions therefore are mandatory. Examples are the Complaints Procedure Directions 1990 (requiring local authorities to establish complaints procedures in adult services to a given format) and the National Assistance Act (Choice of Accommodation) Directions 1992, requiring choice in accommodation arranged by the local authority.

Social Services Practice Guidance is not issued under s.7 and sets out best practice advice on the detail of how services should be managed, rather than what should be provided. It may take the form of a circular or a local authority social services letter (LASSL) or a letter from the Chief Executive of the Social Services Inspectorate. The Managers' Guide and Practitioners' Guide to the implementation of the National Health Service and Community Care Act are examples of such guidance, and are therefore 'relevant matters' to be taken into account when making decisions; again increasing the knowledge base required of both practitioners and managers.

DISCRETIONS AND RIGHTS

Guidance, however, and to a large extent the primary legislation, concentrates on process rather than substantive issues. Though legislative duties are found both in the Children Act 1989 and the National Health Service and Community Care Act 1990 and in related legislation, it is more difficult to argue that these pieces of legislation create substantive rights and that these rights exist for individuals rather than the wider population of people in need. Local authority duties may be subjectively worded so as to give a discretion in defining what is an adequate service. In particular, and following the *Gloucestershire* case (*R. v. Gloucestershire County Council, ex parte Barry* [1997] 2 W.L.R. 459) in the House of Lords, resources, especially financial resources have been held legitimately to define the extent of the duty as well as the means of discharging it. There is no charter of substantive rights relating to service provision, and the quantity of service is never defined. The final arbiters of the limits of a statutory duty are the courts and though interagency working is encouraged in legislation (s.27

Children Act 1989 and s.47 National Health Service and
Community Care Act 1990) the courts have not, on the
whole compelled authorities to take a holistic view of
service provision. Rather, the contrary has happened, with
other agencies: Health; Housing and Social Security being
enabled to use Social Services Departments as a residual
welfare net for continuing care, for homeless families and
unsupported asylum seekers.

MOUNTING A CHALLENGE

Paradoxically, whilst agencies have become more inviolable
concerning the 'big issues', such as the decision to
privatise residential care, or close facilities for children in
need, procedural rights for service users to be involved in
and to challenge individual decisions have increased
through the formalisation of complaints procedures, direct
access to the local government Ombudsman and an
increase in pressure group activity. Almost all challenges to
local authority decision-making lie in the field of public
law. This means that the emphasis is on remedying bad
decision making, rather than offering financial
compensation by way of damages to aggrieved individuals.
However, as we shall see, some systems contain the
opportunity for compensation on an ex gratia basis and a
right of action for breach of statutory duty or negligence in
private law may exceptionally exist to enforce individual
rights and to achieve compensation.

Richards (1996) considers that it is possible to classify
causes of dissatisfaction as relating either to quality or
rationing:

> 'Under the 'quality' heading, the 'problem' may be perceived as the
> quality of service provided, the appropriateness of the services offered
> in a particular case or the professionalism of social services staff. In
> relation to 'rationing' decisions by social services departments, more
> typically the dissatisfaction will relate to the availability of a service,
> i.e. the resources allocated to it and the eligibility criteria used to
> ration it, or to the operation of financial assessment procedures.
> Disputes may also relate to the financial basis on which decisions
> have been made and the legal obligations of the authority.'
>
> (p.147)

Test cases have been brought to obtain an authoritative declaration of the law, though it has to be recognised that legal action is an imperfect instrument for dealing with the complexities of poverty, disability and difficult family relationships. The courts themselves have seen that some situations are too complex for litigation by refusing to accept that there should be liability for individuals or statutory authorities involved in child protection. Here, in the *Bedfordshire* case (*X and Others (Minors) v. Bedfordshire County Council (and conjoined appeals)* [1995] 3 All E.R. 353), policy considerations were made explicit; the desire to avoid defensive practice.

Many opportunities exist within local authority practice, in both child care and adult care, to see quality assurance systems at work through processes of monitoring, inspection and review. The success of systems however is dependent upon good social work practice, knowledge and skills. This includes good management information systems to keep individual workers informed of messages from research and of changes in legislation and guidance. Local authorities own procedures should also be based on open discussion, including consultation of service users, and should be critically evaluated for conformity with national policy and practice guidance.

The purpose of this book is to assist that process of critical evaluation by looking at points within the decision-making process where practice might be criticised as less than adequate to met legal standards. The range of methods by which local authority decisions can be challenged is then explored: this covers use of the complaints procedure; the default powers of the Secretary of State ; referrals to the local government Ombudsman; actions for breach of statutory duty and negligence; and judicial review. The appropriateness and limitations of the different remedies are explored. This book is in essence about anti-oppressive practice in action: about sound and fair decision making; about being open enough to hold one's own practice up to scrutiny; and about recognising that empowerment depends upon the existence of effective and accessible opportunities to challenge the fundamental decisions that local authorities have entrusted to them.

The decision-making process: assessment

Assessment is a core skill of social work, but also a term capable of legal definition. Smale and Tuson (1993) describe three models of assessment;

- the Questioning Model
- the Procedural Model

  and

- the Exchange Model.

The Questioning Model is based on the premise that the professional is expert; and the Procedural Model is managerial in its inception and is based upon the appropriate application of standard criteria. Therefore, only the Exchange Model which is based on negotiation will empower the service user fully as an equal partner in the process of decision making. Assessment is a gateway to service provision, but is also a service, or a duty, in its own right. Thus the duty to assess for community care services under s.47 of the National Health Service and Community Care Act 1990 stands alone, regardless of any service provision decision which may subsequently be made. The duty to investigate where there is reason to suspect that a child may be suffering significant harm under s.47 Children Act 1989 also exists independently of procedures which exist to deal with the outcome of such an investigation. Assessment in the legal sense demands that principles of natural justice, reasonableness and proportionality are taken into account; as such, a knowledge of legal principles in assessment will serve to enhance the implementation of an Exchange Model of assessment.

LEGAL PRINCIPLES IN ASSESSMENT

The following legal principles apply to any assessment,

whatever its legislative source.

- The authority must take all relevant matters, but not irrelevant matters into account. The interviewee should be informed that an assessment is being undertaken. Not only must all the evidence and information provided by the applicant be considered, but any interview should seek to cover all the information that the authority needs in order to make a decision. The person being interviewed should not be left in the position where an adverse inference can be drawn from a failure to disclose material facts.
- If the authority declines to make an assessment, it must give a reason for its decision. An unreasonable delay in making an assessment may amount to maladministration, and may thus be the subject of a referral to the Ombudsman. A tactical response to delay may be to go in to the local authority's complaints procedure at the formal stage to take advantage of the 28 day time limit within that.
- If a local authority has published details of its assessment procedures, it is to be expected that those procedures will be followed. In any event, the procedure must be fair; a standard which is proportionate to the importance of the decision being reached.
- It is a principle of fairness that the applicant should be told of any evidence that is contrary to his case. If expert evidence is provided and the person carrying out the assessment is inclined to disagree with that evidence, they cannot simply set it aside, but must obtain their own expert opinion.
- Services should not be withdrawn without a formal re-assessment, even though reassessment may mean that the same need is now met in a different way.

LOCAL AUTHORITY DUTIES IN ASSESSMENT

Social work assessments deal fundamentally with the person in situation; therefore they are always dynamic and never 'true' (Coulshed, 1991) insofar as they are subjectively influenced by the structure of the agency and the expertise and professional values of the person making the assessment. Limitations may also exist in terms of time available for the assessment and the accessibility of information. There is, for example, a huge difference between a social worker interviewing a patient on a busy public ward for discharge home, and a social worker/ therapist in a child guidance clinic with an assessment span of three months. Nevertheless, the same basic legal principles apply to both. Assessment may have become stylised according to the subject matter of the assessment. An 'Orange Book' assessment in child protection, or an

ASW assessment under the Mental Health Act 1983 and Code of Practice are examples of particularised assessment regimes.

The Managers' Guide to the Interpretation of the Act (1991) outlines six different levels of assessment under the National Health Service and Community Care Act 1990 relating both to the complexity of the presenting problem and the degree of risk involved. Whether the assessment is designated a simple, specialist or comprehensive assessment, the same basic procedural guidelines (above) apply. Section 47(4) of the Community Care Act simply provides that an assessment should be carried out in such a manner and take such form as the local authority consider appropriate. Section 47(1)(a) of the Act provides that the local authority has a duty to carry out an assessment where it appears to the local authority that any person for whom they may provide or arrange for the provision of community care services may be in need of such services. The local authority, having regard to the results of that assessment, shall then decide whether those needs call for the provision by them of any such service (s.47(1)(b)). As subsections (a) and (b) are conceptually distinct, it is clear that the process is a two stage one: first, the assessment of need and secondly a decision on the provision of services. The appearance of need is sufficient to trigger the duty to assess. People in longstay hospitals or in prison may legitimately request an assessment of their need for service provision to be made at some future date following discharge or release. Local authorities which limit the availability of assessment; for example to referrals received from other professionals, may be acting illegally. Those who wish to challenge the local authority, for example through the representations and complaints procedure, on the disparity between their assessed needs and the service provided, may find it useful to emphasise the distinction between the two stages.

All local authority policies, including eligibility criteria and charging policies, are agreed through a committee structure. Local councillors (particularly if they are members of the relevant committee) may help in locating such policies. Richards (1996) advises applicants to check the detail of council policy against any interpretation of that policy by an individual officer. 'Policies' in different area offices within the same authority may in time come to deviate significantly from the agreed policy; in cases of doubt therefore it will be wise to go back to the source.

DEFINITIONS OF NEED

'Need' is the concept used in social policy to access and to gatekeep scarce resources. It is a passive, concept distinguishable from that of rights which is the language of legitimate expectations. For a comprehensive discussion of assessment in social work see Laura Middleton's book in this series: *The Art of Assessment* (1997).

Both the Children Act 1989 and the National Health Service and Community Care Act 1990 (s.17 and s.47 respectively) refer to need as a way in to service provision. There is a difference between the two pieces of legislation insofar as the Community Care Act refers only to a person who 'appears to have a need for community care services', whereas s.17 of the Children Act 1989 is explicit in offering a definition of need. Section 17 has three parts referring to:

i) children who are unlikely to achieve or maintain a reasonable standard of health and development without the provision of services to them (or their families) by the local authority

ii) children whose health or development is likely to be significantly impaired, or further impaired, without the provision of services, and

iii) children who are disabled.

The Children Act 1989 thus appears to offer more scope for objective analysis and challenge, by structuring local authorities' discretion to define what need is.

Local authority responses to children in need have been analysed from both a policy and practitioner perspective by Giller (1993). He found a continuing tendency for policy and practice to be resource-led, with provision for children in need outside the threshold of significant harm being constrained both by the overall availability of resources, and by the perceived demands of higher priority groups under child protection procedures. Social work practice with children in need centred around:

i) the formal recognition of a problem as a 'case' and
ii) assignment of a level of priority to that case

Interventions tended to be highly focused, problem-orientated and practical and because of the pressure of time, inquiries were unlikely to extend beyond the presenting problem. The effect of this is that many needs will go unrecognised and unmet. Research by Aldgate & Tunstill (1995) found that some groups of children including those with mental health needs, young carers and substance abusers were commonly not included as priority groups.

There is no mechanism in Part III of the Children Act 1989 for compelling a local authority to provide services. The complaints procedure will be the usual avenue of redress, and beyond that, use of the default power of the Secretary of State. Judicial review of service provision is limited by the general nature of the duty in s.17 and the scope for subjective interpretation by the local authority. A challenge by way of judicial review was mounted against a decision to run down and close a day nursery in *R. v. Barnet London Borough Council ex parte B* [1994] 1 F.L.R. 592. It was held that the duty under s.18 of the Children Act 1989 to provide day care for children in need under s.17 was a general duty and not one owed to any particular child. Therefore it was for the local authority itself to decide the weight to be given to the circumstances of any individual child in the context of the general range of services provided, and to balance those considerations against its financial and budgetary constraints.

This legitimisation of financial and budgetary constraints both in the planning of services and in assessing the needs of individuals, has been apparent also in the field of community care. To a large extent, the publicity surrounding the coming into force of the National Health Service and Community Care Act 1990 raised false hopes that innovative services would become available to meet a wider range of needs than ever before. In fact the legislation imposes no new substantive duties upon local authorities to provide services that did not already exist under previous legislation. Only the duty to assess is new. The definition of community care services is wholly dependent upon previous legislation; itself a mixture of powers and duties. Section 46 of the Act defines community care services as services provided under:

- Part III of the National Assistance Act 1948 (residential accommodation for people in need of care and attention).
- Section 45 of the Health Services and Public Health Act 1968 (a power to provide services such as day care and meals on wheels specifically for elderly people)
- Section 21 of and Schedule 8 to the National Health Service Act 1977 (a power to make arrangements for the purpose of the prevention of illness and for the care of persons suffering from illness and their aftercare; also a duty to provide home help 'adequate to the needs of the area', and a power to provide laundry services.)
- Section 117 of the Mental Health Act 1983 (aftercare duties in respect of people detained, inter alia, under s.3)

Section 47(2) of the National Health Service and Community Care Act 1990 makes particular reference to people with a disability (s.47(2)) whose needs are to be assessed under s.4 of the Disabled Persons (Services, Consultation and Representation) Act 1986 for services available under the Chronically Sick and Disabled Persons Act 1970; a 'shopping list' of services which includes access to day care, aids and adaptations, telephone installation and domiciliary services. Prior to the Gloucestershire decision (1997) it was thought to be an advantage to emphasise disability (which includes mental illness), on the assumption that under the Chronically Sick and Disabled Persons Act 1970 there was an unequivocal duty to meet assessed needs. It now appears that this is not the case.

NEEDS, SERVICES AND RESOURCES

Although the Policy Guidance (1990) emphasises throughout the legislative mandate for 'needs led' assessment, this is not the same as 'user led' assessment. In other words, what people say they want or would like may not be the service which the local authority will provide. The Managers' Guide (1991) is clear about where it thinks the power of definition will lie (and this is likely now to be accepted by the courts as a proper statement of the legal position). Addressing the definition of need, paras. 12 and 13 of the Guide say:

> Need is a dynamic concept, the definition of which will vary over time in accordance with:
> - Changes in national legislation
> - Changes in local policy
> - The availability of resources
> - The patterns of local demand

Need is thus a relative concept. In the context of community care, need has to be defined at the local level. That definition sets limits to the discretion of practitioners in accessing resources.

Braye & Preston-Shoot (1994) have drawn attention to the triangulation of needs, services and resources which lead to the logical conundrum that a need may be defined as non-existent in circumstances where there are no resources to meet that need. It was just this sort of argument that was the focus of the dispute in the Gloucestershire cases. The political background to these cases was a decision by Gloucestershire Council to withdraw cleaning and laundry services from 1,500 disabled people in their area by the sending a standard letter, and without formal reassessment. Certain aggrieved individuals with support from RADAR challenged this decision by way of judicial review. At first instance, they were successful in challenging the legality of withdrawing a service without assessment, and in the Court of Appeal, a majority judgement upheld their argument that resource constraints could not affect the existence of the duty to meet an apparent need. The case then went to the House of Lords which reversed the decision of the Court of Appeal and (by a majority) decided that resources were a valid consideration in the assessment of need as well as in the provision of resources and that this was as true of assessment for services under the Chronically Sick and Disabled Persons Act 1970, as it was of assessment under the National Health Service and Community Care Act 1990.

The effect of this judgement is to legitimise the use of eligibility criteria at the assessment stage as well as at the service provision stage and to considerably narrow the scope for arguing that 'unmet need' can exist. It should not however exclude from assessment those people who frame their request wrongly in terms of an ineligible service. An example would be a request for domestic cleaning which the local authority did not provide. The fact that a particular service, was not commonly available, should not be regarded as discharging the local authority's general duty under s.47 National Health Service and Community Care Act 1990 to assess the need for community care services. Other needs might well arise in the course of such an assessment. In particular, health care needs and housing needs are specifically addressed within s.47. A person with a particular medical need for a clean environment might well meet the local authority's eligibility criteria for domestic cleaning. Not to take those needs into account would be a neglect of relevant matters sufficient to challenge the legality of the assessment.

UNMET NEED

There have been difficulties (probably now resolved as a consequence of the Gloucestershire case), over the legal implications of recording unmet need. The Practice Guidance (para. 4.37) advises that unmet need be recorded in a care plan. Clements (1996) interprets 'unmet need' in this sense as meaning simply services that the local authority would provide if it had more resources available and therefore could afford more liberal eligibility criteria: logically it would be impossible for it to mean 'services which the authority had failed to provide even when it was under an obligation to do so', as this would clearly be illegal. Herbert Laming, Chief Inspector of the Social Services Inspectorate was not, however, so confident that local authorities would properly make this distinction: in the famous Laming Letter of 1992 (CI(92)34) he counselled local authorities against recording unmet need on an individual basis (lest it should form the basis of a legal challenge) and instead advocated aggregating unmet need so as to inform the policy making process. Many local authorities do not record unmet need individually; the Gloucestershire judgement in legitimising eligibility criteria appears however to remove the legal jeopardy in doing so. Measuring unmet need in the aggregate remains important for service planning in the future and the Practitioners' Guide (para. 4.32) urges local authorities to do this.

Care planning

The care plan which is produced following the process of assessment is a crucial document which specifies what it is going to be done, by whom and when. The Policy Guidance (1990, para. 3.24) is explicit about what the care plan should contain:

- The needs to be met
- The services to be provided or arranged
- The objectives of the intervention

Where agreement between all parties is not possible, the points of difference should be recorded (para. 3.25); it will be important to emphasise such agreements or disagreements if the care plan is later challenged. The Policy Guidance must be followed unless there is good reason to depart from it 'articulated in the course of some identifiable decision-making process, even if not in the care plan itself': *R. v. Islington London Borough Council, ex parte Rixon*, The Times, April 17, 1996. In the Rixon case, the local authority was held to have produced an inadequate care plan which did not properly address the social and educational needs of Mr Rixon. It had also not followed the format laid down in the Practitioners' Guide; and although this was not formally binding, there was an assumption that it would be 'conscientiously' taken into account.

CARE PLANNING IN THE GUIDANCE

Both the Policy Guidance and the Practitioners' Guide emphasise that assessment should be needs led, and, following on from this, that care planning should not be seen as matching needs with resources 'off the shelf' but as an opportunity to rethink service provision for a particular individual (para. 4.12, Practitioners' Guide). A proper care plan should:

---

1. target any interventions as clearly as possible on the identified need, in response to an understanding of the individual's daily pattern of living.
2. refer to the level of risk agreed with users and carers at the assessment stage, in compliance with agency guidelines on risktaking.
3. reconcile preferences and resources, with users being informed of their right to make representations under the complaints procedure.
4. be costed, and the user advised in writing of any charges involved before the care plan is agreed.
5. identify unmet needs (which themselves are prioritised)
6. fix a date for the first review

A care plan is well described in the Practitioners' Guide (para. 4.39) as a 'blueprint for action'; and should be set out in 'concise written form' (para. 4.37). It describes the responsibilities of agencies contributing to the delivery of the plan and emphasises the importance of specifying how the attainment of objectives might be measured. Any points of difference between the user, carer, care planning practitioner or other agency should be noted. Having completed the care plan, the practitioner should identify any assessed need which it has not been able to address, and the reasons for this. This information should be fed back for service planning and quality assurance. The service user should be given a copy of the care plan, which he may be asked to sign.

COMMISSIONING AND PURCHASING SERVICES

When the question is one of commissioning or purchasing services to meet assessed need, the local authority can exercise its own discretion in how it chooses to meet that need, provided it acts with flexibility in exceptional cases. Therefore, an assessment of the need for 24 hour care can result in a service provision decision that this is only available in residential or nursing home care (as appropriate). The service user cannot choose to receive that care at home. The principle of choice, and the emphasis on the primacy of care in the community are thus subordinated to issues of resources. Local authorities (and health authorities) commonly allow for up to fourteen hours per week of domiciliary care, before the cost of such care exceeds their contribution to a residential placement. In the *Lancashire* case:*R. v Lancashire County Council, ex parte RADAR and Gilpin* (1996) The Times, July, 12, 1996, the applicant was unsuccessful in her attempt to use judicial review to challenge precisely such a decision that nursing home care was the appropriate response to the needs of her mother (now deceased). Gordon and Mackintosh (1996) are critical of this decision insofar as it may have been based on an inadequate assessment of the elderly person's psychological needs, and the effect on her wellbeing of a precipitate move into nursing home care. For this and other disputes regarding the proposed package of care, they suggest attention should be given to the scope and adequacy of the assessment.

THE 'DIRECTION ON CHOICE'

Choice of placement within residential care should be made available under the National Assistance Act 1948 (Choice of Accommodation) Directions 1992 and LAC 92(27) which introduce the concept of 'preferred accommodation'. The Directions seek to meet the concern that persons who are dependent upon local authority funding will lose choice and will simply be 'placed' in accommodation by the local authority. The Directions state that if an individual concerned expresses a preference for particular accommodation ('preferred accommodation') within the UK the authority must arrange for care in that accommodation provided

- the accommodation is suitable in relation to the individual's assessed needs (which of course includes psychological needs) and may also (according to accompanying guidance) include a need to move to another part of the country to be near a relative.
- to do so would not cost the authority more than it would usually expect to pay for accommodation for someone with the individual's assessed needs.
- the accommodation is available
- the person in charge of the accommodation is willing to provide accommodation subject to the authority's usual terms and conditions for such accommodation.

If a resident requests it, the authority must also arrange for care in accommodation more expensive than it would normally fund provided there is a third party willing and able to pay the difference between the cost the authority would usually expect to pay and the actual cost of the accommodation. The Direction applies to those already in residential care seeking to transfer, as well as to new applicants and to respite as well as permanent care. The Guidance (LAC (92)27)) which accompanies the Direction describes it (para. 3) 'as intended to formalise the best practice which most authorities would in any case have adopted.' Giving effect to 'preferred accommodation' is a legal duty, not dependent upon resources; it is important therefore that practitioners ensure its implementation.

CHALLENGING THE CARE PLAN

The Policy Guidance (1990) stipulates that all users in receipt of a continuing service should have a written care plan, even if only a brief one, which defines the user's needs and the objectives to be met by any service provider. Though a care plan is not legally a contract, it may be used as evidence in the consideration of a complaint (Practitioners' Guide para. 4.38). Mandamus will be available (see the chapter on judicial review) to compel a reluctant local authority to produce a satisfactory care plan. In *R. v. Sutton London Borough Council, ex parte Tucker* C.O. 1075- 96, October 29, 1996, the Divisional Court compelled the local authority to produce within 21 days a care plan. The applicant's daughter had, in the absence of a care plan, remained in hospital despite an assessment that acknowledged her need for a placement in shared accommodation in the community. The situation had been allowed to drift and no suitable accommodation had been identified. The decision in this case was an endorsement of the stance taken in the *Rixon* case: *R. v Islington London Borough Council, ex parte Rixon* [1996] 5 CL 375 that the preparation of a care plan in accordance with the guidance was an imperative for planning longterm needs, and illustrates how effective judicial review can be in forcing local authorities to act.

Decision-making in respect of children in the care system will involve scrutiny of the local authority's care plan by the courts. The extent to which the courts are able to control local authority decision-making has proved

contentious. Wall J. in *Re J (Minors) (Care: Plan)* [1994] 1
F.L.R. 253 analysed thus the division of responsibility
between the court and the local authority in the making
and implementation of a care order following the Children
Act 1989:

- the court may retain control over the case (by use of interim orders) in order to acquire as much information as is available before a 'passing over of responsibility'.
- the care plan should address all the matters set out in vol. 3 Chapter 2 para. 2.62 of the Regulations and Guidance (Family Placements) relating to the care of the child. This includes arrangements for contact; the likely duration of the placement; and the extent to which the wishes and feeling of the child and his parents have been acted upon. The care plan should also contain the child and his family's social history, and an identification of the child's needs including needs relating to his race, culture and religion or language, and special educational or health needs.
- the obligation placed upon the court to regard the welfare of the child as paramount, will entitle the court to refuse to make a care order if it is not satisfied that the local authority's care plan is in the best interests of the child

This proactive stance by the courts had already be seen in
re B (Minors) (Care: Contact: Local Authority's Plans)
[1993] 1 F.L.R. 543, where the court did not shrink from
disrupting the settled plans of the local authority for the
adoption of two children by giving consideration to the
mother's application for contact. A local authority which
implements its original plan poorly by delay in making a
suitable placement may therefore find itself open to this
sort of challenge. This is very different from the
noninterventionist stand taken by the courts in pre-
Children Act 1989 cases. Explicitly, it seeks to compensate
for the loss of the wardship jurisdiction, one advantage of
which was to monitor a tendency for cases to drift without
formal review. The emphasis on the care plan also reflects
the reality that in the majority of cases the threshold
criteria for the making of a care order are conceded, and it
is the local authority's plans that then assume the greater
importance, particularly in respect of contact and
adoption.

The highwater mark of intervention has, however, been
re C [1997] 1 F.L.R. 1; a decision of the House of Lords.

There it was accepted that the court has power under an interim care order to direct where the assessment of the child should take place (in this case, in a residential establishment paid for by the local authority). Assessment in the child's own home would be equally available. The conclusion to be drawn from this line of cases is that the courts have lost some confidence in the ability of the local authority efficiently to assess and safeguard the welfare of the child. Whether the judiciary, in terms of training, resources and time available for reflection can analyse the needs of the child as accurately as other professionals is discussed by Carole Smith in the BAAF Review 1995/6.

COOPERATION BETWEEN AUTHORITIES

Both the Children Act 1989 and the National Health Service and Community Care Act 1990 are predicated on the assumption that cooperation between authorities in the social care field is important and will happen. Cooperation however is not always easy to achieve and is hampered by different professional perspectives and, more fundamentally, by the different legal mandates within which social services, health, housing, and education – to name the major players in the field – are constrained to work. On the whole, when legal challenges have happened to seek to enforce working together, the result has been to define even more stringently the particular responsibilities of individual agencies.

In the case of children, Aldgate and Simmonds (1988) suggest that it is not the presence of one particular problem, but their range that is likely to affect a child's wellbeing. Section 27 of the Children Act 1989 empowers social services departments to request assistance from other statutory agencies, who are expected to respond positively to such a request if it is within their remit to do so. The limits of this cooperation were tested *R. v. Northavon District Council, ex parte Smith* [1994] 3 W.L.R. 403 in which the Social Services Department requested accommodation from the local housing authority for a travelling family whose children were 'in need' under s.17. The housing authority refused, as the family were intentionally homeless. The dispute between the two authorities was taken to judicial review which upheld the right of the housing authority ultimately to reject the representations made to it and to confine itself to statutory housing responsibilities and priorities contained therein. Although the court in that case frowned upon the use of judicial review to settle disputes between public authorities, it has been further used in subsequent cases to resolve jurisdictional issues. In *R. v. Lincolnshire County Council, ex parte Atkinson and others* August 31, 1995, (discussed by Clements (1997)) the High Court held that the power given by Part V of the Criminal Justice and Public Order Act 1994 to evict travellers did not remove the local authority's social welfare duties towards vulnerable people: the duty to provide for such people properly fell upon the social services department; it could not fall elsewhere as the same piece of legislation had abolished the specific duty to provide council sites for gypsics within each area

Clements (1997) sees social services departments being used increasingly as overstretched safety nets for other agencies' rejections. In effect a new poor law is being created out of considerations of 'common humanity' by the judiciary who are using the flexibility inherent in the National Assistance Act 1948 and the Children Act 1989 to avoid the draconian effect of some recent legislation. The highwatermark of this trend was the decision of the Court of Appeal in *R. v. Hammersmith and Fulham London Borough Council, ex parte M* The Times, February, 19, 1997 (the asylum seekers case). Parliament had through legislation excluded substantial numbers of asylum seekers from a right to income support or public housing assistance by the Asylum and Immigration Act of the previous year. Against this background, the court interpreted s.21(1) of the National Assistance Act 1948 as imposing a duty upon local authorities (through their Social Services Committee) to provide services to individuals in extreme circumstances who were in need of 'care and attention' which was not otherwise available to them. Lord Woolf MR referred in that case to the National Assistance Act 1948 as an Act which was 'always speaking'; accordingly, it should be construed by continuously updating its wording to allow for changes since the Act was written. More reinterpretation of Social Services

Departments' duties may therefore be yet to come.

The Children Act 1989, only recently written, has also had its meaning stretched to encompass rehousing families which contain children in need. The case referred to, *R. Tower Hamlets London Borough Council, ex parte Bradford* (discussed by Luke Clements in Community Care 13-19 February 1997 pp 28-29) is an interesting example of interlocking needs and statutory obligations. The family comprised Mr and Mrs Bradford and their 11 year old son Simon. Mrs Bradford was severely disabled, suffering several epileptic fits a day, and her son had special educational needs. They were socially isolated and had suffered harassment from neighbours. The family applied for a housing transfer and their solicitors wrote to Tower Hamlets requesting that a comprehensive assessment be carried out under the National Health Service and Community Care Act 1990, the Chronically Sick and Disabled Persons Act 1970 and the Children Act 1989. The community care assessment concluded that Mrs Bradford's needs were insufficient to justify rehousing the family. The focus therefore shifted to the Children Act assessment. Kay. J. concluded that the authority had shown a 'fundamental misunderstanding' of their powers in relation to rehousing under the Children Act – despite the fact that it has no housing stock, assessment of families' housing needs was within the purview of the Act. Comprehensive assessments under the Children Act 1989 as well as the National Health Service and Community Care Act 1990 must therefore include housing issues within their scope, and it appears as if housing vulnerable people is rapidly becoming a Social Services Department responsibility.

Monitoring and review

The final stages of the care management process are monitoring and review. Monitoring describes the process of overseeing the care plan, whereas review is the term most often used to describe a single formal event when the situation is scrutinised and evaluated. The duty under s.47(1) of the National Health Service and Community Care Act 1990 to carry out an assessment is a continuing duty whenever there is an apparent need for community care services. Any significant changes in circumstances therefore should lead to reassessment. The same legal principles apply to reassessment as they do to the original assessment (see p. 8 above). a local authority's unreasonable refusal to reassess would be challengeable through the complaints procedure and by way of judicial review. Though there is no statutory duty to review the provision of community care services, both policy and practice guidance assume that this will be done.

WITHDRAWAL OF COMMUNITY CARE SERVICES

Withdrawal of community care services without reassessment is unlawful; this principle established in the Court of Appeal in Gloucestershire case was not overturned on appeal to the House of Lords. Where an entire service is withdrawn (and this is not an unusual scenario, given the trend towards privatisation of the local authority's own Part III provision), full consultation of those affected is required; though this extend may extend only to residents as a class, and not to each individual resident: *R. v. Devon County Council, ex parte Baker* [1995] 1 All E.R. 73. Such consultation however must be timely; well informed; and regarded seriously.

REVIEWS UNDER THE CHILDREN ACT 1989

Regular reviews of children looked after by the local authority are a legislative requirement under s.28 Children

Act 1989. Reviews are a coming together of all those with significant responsibilities for the child; the child and its parents should also attend, and be given help and support to participate in the decision-making and to make sure that their views are known (s.26). The duty under s.22 to take into account the wishes and feelings of the child are also of relevance to reviews. Duties of consultation, participation, and communication are explicitly set out in the Review of Children's Cases Regulations 1991, and are thus a legal requirement. This means that judicial review may lie if consultation is disregarded or treated cursorily. Section 22(5) requires the local authority to give due consideration to the child's religious persuasion, racial origin and cultural and linguistic background. The Act thus specifies what 'relevant matters' for the purpose of judicial review are to be. Section 22 is a central part of the Act to invoke when seeking to keep the local authority to its statutory brief in relation to children they are looking after or proposing to look after.

Volume 3 of the Guidance on the Children Act is explicit that the use of a different name for what in effect is a statutory review, cannot be used by the local authority to avoid its particular obligations under s.26 and the Regulations. Para. 8.3 of the Guidance states:

> *'any meeting which is convened for the purpose of considering that child's case in connection with any aspect of the review of that case falls within the scope of these regulations. Whether such a meeting is called a planning meeting or a review or a review meeting will not determine whether it is in fact part of a review. This will depend upon the purpose for which the meeting is convened.'*

Judicial review of the review function in child care cases would be based upon the assumption that a 'review' is a decision-making body. Thoburn (1986) questions this assumption that a review is a decision-making meeting; and discusses the alternative view that it is a quality control mechanism. The function of a review is then to ensure that an effective service is being offered in the daytoday task of social work which is in line with the policy of the local authority, and appropriate to the needs of the individual case. It is of course the 'little' decisions in social work that really make the difference to how situations develop: Thoburn gives examples of these in the decision whether or not to pay fares to enable parents to visit; what response to make if a visit is cancelled by parents or foster carers; or whether to hold a meeting with granny to discuss whether she could care for the child. The attitudes and actions of individual social workers will often pass without scrutiny, and will never become the subject of major challenges, but they have a potent influence on the quality of the child's experience of care.

Quality assurance

Quality assurance and quality control operate as processes through which standards of service are set and maintained. Quality assurance is the term which is used to refer to systems which ensure that concern for quality is designed and built into service specifications: quality control refers to processes of verification such as monitoring, audit and inspection which establish whether or not standards are being achieved. 'Total quality management' stresses the importance of creating a culture in which concern for quality is an integral part of service delivery (DoH, 1992).

This procedural approach to quality management of course does not answer the question of who defines what quality is in any particular service. Is it to be the service user, the commissioner of that service (the local authority), or the provider of the service? Having one's voice heard means being involved in the setting of standards, and having accessible forms of redress if something goes wrong.

DEFINITION OF TERMS

Concern for quality may be pursued with four primary functions in mind. (DoH, 1993)

- to demonstrate value for money;
- to demonstrate achievement of purpose;
- to improve the experience of the service user;
- to act as an integrating device in the management of departmental change.

Measures of outcome may be different for each of these objectives; for example, a value for money service may do nothing to improve the subjective experience of the service user. Intervention strategies may be linked only loosely to a statement of desired outcomes; Giller (1993) found that this was true of service provision for children in need: 'success' is difficult to measure if the desired outcome is not clearly specified. Evaluation of a service is particularly difficult when that service is personal care, given the constraints on users and carers expressing dissatisfaction with a service upon which they are dependent.

TRENDS WITHIN QUALITY ASSURANCE

A number of trends are discernible within the development of quality assurance and quality control. These are:

1 The use of national or local standards documents directed to quality but not quantity of service; and establishing minimum yardsticks for good administrative practice over such matters as response times, staff accountability and access to information. Examples are the Patients' Charter, the Citizens' Charter and local Community Care Charters and standards documents produced by the Social Services Inspectorate and Audit Commission.
2 The development of Community Care Plans and Children's Services Plans which describe priorities between and within services.
3 Debate around the continued desirability of registration as a means of quality assurance within a statutory framework. The issues are set out in the Burgner Report (1996).
4 A growth in accreditation, rather than regulation, with reliance placed on service providers' own internal quality assurance systems.
5 Standard setting through contract compliance mechanisms.
6 The structuring within organisations of professional discretion through the increased use of standard form assessments and eligibility criteria: monitoring being carried out through peer group or managerial audit or inspection.

A number of instruments do exist for measuring quality in service provision. Some local authorities, most notably Norfolk and Gloucestershire have adopted the British Standards Institute's BS5750 for use in social care agencies by modifying the concepts of 'fitness for purpose' and 'safety in use' contained therein to include consumer perspectives. Improved outcomes for users is identified by the DoH Report 'Committed to Quality' in 1992 as the prime aim of quality assurance approaches. The report goes on to describe a joint project between Humberside Social Services Department and East Yorkshire Health Authority to set standards for each of their client groups by coopting a 'diagonal slice' (meaning people involved in each of those client groups at all levels of the organisation) including senior, middle and front line managers, professionals, practitioners and ancillary workers, who combine with

users to form a project team. The results are used to set
unit targets for each quality standard (Lynch & Pope, 1990).

CONTRACTS WITH THE INDEPENDENT SECTOR

The process of care planning also involves issues of quality.
Monitoring and evaluating contracts is a crucial element in
the contracting process. A variety of types of contract may
coexist: individual or spot contracts; block contracts and
cost and volume contracts. Each of these contracts
combines different risks for the provider, and varying
degrees of flexibility for the purchaser. The use that is
made of each of them will depend upon the amount of
competition in the market and the policies of the local
authority. In the selection of wouldbe contractors there is
no obligation for the local authority to act in compliance
with the rules of natural justice, or to act consistently; a
statement of council policy on the selection of applicants
will not amount to an 'offer' in the contractual sense: *R. v.
Knowsley Borough Council, ex parte Maguire and Others*
(1992) 90 L.G.R. 653. For an overview of contractual issues
see 'Diversification and the Independent Sector' (DoH,
1993); at a minimum local authority contracts should cover:

1 a description of the type of service to be provided and a statement of the aims
and objectives to be achieved;
2 a statement of the quality of care expected;
3 obligations of the care provider in respect of health and safety matters and
antidiscriminatory practice;
4 the complaints procedure that exists for the benefit of the consumer of the
service;
5 dispute resolution procedures; and
6 the arrangements for contract monitoring and review.

It has been established that local authorities can introduce
into their contracts with private providers terms which are
more stringent than basic legal requirements under
sources of legislation other than the National Health
Service and Community Care Act 1990. For example, a
residential care home which is registered (as it must be)
under the Registered Homes Act 1984, will be required to
conform to certain conditions relating to the numbers,
ages, sex and category of persons to be registered. In

addition, the local authority may impose its own requirements on such matters as provision of single rooms and adequacy of staffing levels. Any general policy in relation to registration must be publicly stated, but may not be applied as a matter of routine without considering the circumstances of each individual case; *Isle of Wight County Council v. Humphreys* (1992) 90 L.G.R. 186. However, in contracting with the independent sector to provide residential care services, the local authority may legitimately include contract terms which are more stringent than the home's basic registration requirement. There is no entitlement for a residential home to have its name placed upon an approved list of providers, as this is purely a matter of private contract law.

CONSUMER REDRESS

The service user is not well protected legally if something goes wrong in the execution of the contract. Unless the service user themselves is made a party to the contract, ordinary principles of contract law means that they cannot sue on the contract, though there may be an action in negligence against the provider if there is a breach of duty of care (and possibly also against the local authority which has arranged the care). Richards (1996) suggests that it will be less trouble to ask the local authority to take its own action against an unsatisfactory provider and to use the complaints procedure against the local authority for any failure to do so. It is important therefore that service specifications offer adequate protection to both user and provider. The local authority may also terminate the contract that it has with a particular provider, even though a different provider is less well able to meet the users needs. Cragg (1996) gives an example of this in the case of a man with a learning disability who was provided with a male facilitator; the service provider was then changed and female staff were used. The service user objected and began judicial review proceedings against the local authority. He did not succeed; the care provided still met his basic needs, and the local authority's freedom to contract within their resources would not be constrained by individual preferences. But as Day et al (1996) conclude in their study of regulatory regimes; giving service users a 'voice' in setting standards should as a matter of principle be balanced by an opportunity to 'exit' the system if the service provided is not acceptable to the individual user. Direct payments may in future enable some users to exit the system; however, the scheme outlined in the Direct Payments Act 1996 is discretionary and those dependent upon local authority resources will still have their needs and costs balanced for them by the local authority.

INSPECTION UNITS

The Policy Guidance (1990) required local authorities to set up Inspection Units with responsibility for fulfilling the authority's statutory duties in relation to the registration and inspection of services. These units are to be 'free standing' i.e. separate from line management, in order that they can also assume responsibility for inspecting the local authority's own services. The White Paper on Social Services (1997) has recommended that this independence should be emphasised still further by locating Inspection Units still within local government, but elsewhere than in the Social Services Department, possibly within Trading Standards.

Registration as a means of quality assurance and standard setting has a long history dating back to the Nursing Homes Act of 1927. A dual system now operates under which residential care homes are registered and inspected by the local authority and nursing homes by the health authority, though dual registration is possible and combined local authority/health authority units do exist. The relevant legislation is now the Residential Homes Act 1984, and regulations. The registration and inspection of residential care faces problems common to all regulatory systems: policing versus consultancy; rules versus discretion; stringency versus accommodation. Paradoxically, some aspects of the system may be intended to pose difficulties.

The present system is in many cases overloaded; the Social Services Inspectorate itself found that nine of the 19 inspection

> 'registration is deliberately designed as an obstacle course (a sort of initiation ceremony) that forces prospective home owners to demonstrate that they are 'fit persons', that their plans meet local guidelines and that they know what is expected of them'. **(Day et al, 1996)**

units included in its (1995) survey had failed to meet the target of twice yearly inspections. Day 's (1996) research however highlighted inconsistencies between inspection units with regard to the number of staff and the size of the budget proportionate to the number of homes to be inspected. Considerable variation in standards and their interpretation were seen even within the same unit. It was these sorts of inconsistencies that irritated service providers, who were increasingly moving towards a common set of expectations with the regulatory bodies about good practice. Unresolved disputes between home owners and managers and inspection unit staff if based on maladministration may be referred to the Ombudsman. Appeals against the refusal or cancellation of registration are dealt with by registered homes tribunals. But, as with many administrative systems, there is a judicial forum in reserve to enable local authorities to act more quickly than the protracted period (at least three months, and possibly 18 months) normally allowed for the cancellation of registration. This is s.11 of the Registered Homes Act 1984 whereby the local authority may apply, ex parte if necessary, to a magistrates court for the immediate cancellation of registration.

A challenge to the registration regime for childminders has confirmed a principle already established by the registered homes tribunals in respect of residential care homes; that is, that the local authority cannot adopt a blanket policy to determine the 'fitness' or otherwise of the person seeking registration. In the case of *Sutton London Borough Council v. Davis* [1994] 2 W.L.R. 721 the policy of the local authority to refuse registration to any person who would not agree not to smack a child in their care was successfully challenged by way of judicial review. Each applicant for registration has to be considered on their overall merits. Therefore general requirements as to necessary qualifications (Dip SW or RGN, for example) would be unlawful. The existence of discretion (and the courts' willingness to support it) may therefore be a structural barrier to the evolution of good professional practice. Unless that practice is contained in regulations and guidance it will not be of persuasive authority in determining legal issues.

Remedies: local authority complaints procedures

Prior to the Children Act 1989 and the National Health Service and Community Care Act 1990, local authority complaints procedures were ad hoc and variable; not every authority had a complaints procedure, and there was no standard pattern. The Children Act 1989 and the National Health Service and Community Care Act 1990 specify standard complaints procedures to be followed by all authorities in child care and community care matters. The procedures are separate, but parallel, though there are some differences between the two procedures, most notably that the Children Act 1989 procedures involve an independent element at an earlier stage. 'National Standards' are far from having been achieved; the Social Services Inspectorate Inspection of Complaints Procedures in Local Authority Social Services Departments (Third Overview Report 1996) confirmed earlier findings that considerable differences in process and performance between authorities still existed.

- The complaints procedure is normally the first route to take in challenging local authority decisions
- The effectiveness of the system is dependent upon people knowing about and being assisted to use the procedures
- There is no requirement to pay compensation, though some authorities will do so.

Complaints procedures should be kept separate from grievance procedures and disciplinary procedures which concern internal staffing matters. The Policy Guidance on the implementation of the National Health Service and Community Care Act 1990 sees complaints procedures as an integral part of the process of care management; an assessment, or service provision decision should itself contain reference to the local authority's complaints procedure and information from the complaints procedure about how systems are working should be fed back into the process of service planning. The complaints procedure is intended to be the primary route by which local authority decisions are challenged. Other avenues of redress: judicial review; recourse to the Ombudsman; actions for breach of statutory duty and default powers on the whole operate on the assumption that the complaints procedure of the local authority has been exhausted. Paradoxically, these other systems themselves have been fruitful sources of evidence that deficiencies within the complaints procedure itself exist, whether those faults are structural or operational.

Section 50 of the National Health Service and Community Care Act 1990 requires all local authorities to set up representations and complaints procedures for adult services; this section came into force on 1st April 1991 and applies to all matters arising after that time. A common format is laid down in the Policy Guidance; Complaints Procedure Directions 1990; 'The Right to Complain' DoH 1991 (s.7 Guidance) and 'Notes on Good Practice' Social Services Inspectorate 1995. Section 26 of the Children Act 1989 requires local authorities to set up procedures for considering representations (including complaints) about childrens services. The Representations Procedure (Children) Regulations (1991) came into force 14th October 1991. The Social Services Inspectorate has also produced three overview reports on the operation of local authority complaints procedures in 1993, 1994 and 1996. Therefore there is a good deal of information available to assist those involved in applying the procedures and those who use them.

WHO MAY COMPLAIN

Under the National Health Service and Community Care Act 1990 complaints must relate to the local authority's social service functions, and must be made by and in respect of a 'qualifying individual'. A person is a qualifying individual if

- A local authority has a power or a duty to provide, or secure the provision of a social service for him; and
- His need or possible need for such a service has (by whatever means) come to the attention of the authority. Carers are now included within the definition by virtue of the Carers (Recognition and Services) Act 1995.

Children Act procedures contain different qualifying conditions. Under s.26(3) of the Children Act 1989 any of the following may make representations or complaints.

- children in need or looked after by the local authority;
- their parents;
- persons with parental responsibility;
- any local authority foster parent;
- any such other person as the local authority consider has a sufficient interest in the child's welfare

Complaints must relate only to matters within Part III of the Act (children in need); Parts IV and V relating to child protection are excluded from the statutory scheme. However, some Area Child Protection Committees have developed their own procedures for dealing with such complaints. Local authorities may, at their discretion deal with representations or complaints falling outside these parameters, but are free to reject anonymous or generalised complaints.

STAGES IN THE HANDLING OF A COMPLAINT

There are three stages in the handing of a complaint:

1 **The informal or problem-solving stage;**
2 **The formal or registration stage; and**
3 **The review stage.**

The authority should also appoint a 'designated officer' to oversee the complaints procedure as a whole .

The informal stage operates by way of reference back to the relevant worker or manager. However, the fact that this stage is informal does not mean that it is 'casual' and there may be a need, recognised in 'The Right to Complain' to involve someone who is not connected with the immediate problem to help resolve it. If the problem cannot be satisfactorily resolved at this stage, then the complainant has the right to move onto the next, and formal, stage for which the complaint must be made in writing to the Designated Complaints Officer. At this stage the complaint will be investigated and a report, with recommendations, will be made to the Designated Complaints Officer. There is no requirement that the full report should be disclosed to the complainant, but good practice (para. 4.13 of the Right to Complain) would indicate that this should happen, and that reasons should be given for the decision that is reached. It is at this stage that time limits come into play; the Complaints Procedure Directions require a response to be formulated within 28 days of the receipt of the complaint, or if this is not possible, an explanation should be given and the complainant told when he can expect a response, which in any case must be within three months.

The complainant may wish to prepare his case by getting independent reports, for example, on his medical condition. If the local authority wish to challenge the content of these reports they must produce their own rebutting evidence. A psychologist's report on the cognitive abilities of people with Down's syndrome was highly effective in the Mark Hazell case (see below) and persuaded the review panel that the particular type of residential care to which Mark had committed himself was a need and not a preference. It will nearly always be useful to have sight of the social services file; in which case advance notice will need to be given as the local authority has 40 days under the Access to Personal Files Act within which to produce the file and the complaints procedure resolution time is 28 days. Reference to Citizen Charter Standards and Community Care Charter Standards may also indicate how far the local authority has deviated from standards of good administration in dealing with cases quickly and efficiently even though these standards are not directly enforceable.

If the complainant remains dissatisfied with the result he has the right to request that the matter should be referred to a panel for review. The panel has to meet within 28 days when it holds an oral hearing and makes recommendations which are recorded in writing within 24 hours of the meeting. The panel is also required to record the reasons for their recommendations in writing, and to send copies to the local authority; the complainant, if appropriate; the person whose behalf the representations were made; and any other person who the local authority considers has sufficient interest in the case.

The procedure at the review stage is intended to be administratively similar under both the Children Act 1989 and the National Health Service and Community Care Act 1990; indeed, the two procedures might well merge at this point. The review panel should comprise three people, with an 'independent person' as chair. Other members may be senior managers of the authority, or local councillors, or they too may be independent persons. Independent persons are expected to have experience relevant to the subject matter of the complaint; and the list from which they are taken should reflect the ethnic makeup of the local population and should be prepared in consultation with voluntary agencies and other local groups. In Community Care Act cases where an Independent Person has not been involved at the formal investigatory stage, the panel will act de novo; that is it will consider afresh all the evidence from the beginning of the complaints procedure. The meeting of the review panel should be conducted as informally as possible, but with due regard to confidentiality. There is a right to make both written and oral submissions to the panel. Complainants should be given the opportunity to be accompanied by another person who would be entitled to be present at the whole meeting and to speak on their behalf; however, this person should not be a barrister or solicitor acting in a professional capacity. Legal advice in appropriate cases may be obtained through the Green Form Scheme. An extension may be granted for a solicitor to act as a 'McKenzie friend' to give advice during the hearing and to take notes. The Public Law Project (1994) gives further details. Highly complex legal arguments are not suitable for resolution by the complaints procedure; in such cases, the complainant may go straight to judicial review.

CHALLENGES TO THE COMPLAINTS PROCEDURE

The decision of the complaints review panel is by way of a recommendation to the Director of Social Services and to the Social Services Committee, who have a discretion whether or not to accept the recommendation. This discretion, however, is subject to judicial review, as is the proper exercise of the whole of the remainder of the complaints process. Limits on the discretion of the Social Services Committee to reject the review panel's recommendation were examined by Henry J. in *R. v. Avon County Council ex parte Mark Hazell* [1994] 2 F.L.R. 1006; (for a discussion of the case see the article by Catriona Marchant, in Community Care, July 15, 1993 p.18). The case concerned Mark, a young man of 22 with Down's syndrome whose preferred placement was with the Home Farm Trust, rather than the alternative residential accommodation favoured by the local authority. On hearing evidence that the Home Farm Trust was the only placement that would meet Mark's psychological needs, the review panel held in his favour; their recommendation was not accepted by the local authority. Henry J. held that as a general principle of law, the review panel's recommendation could not be overturned without substantial reason, as that body was the 'obvious and intended forum' for a detailed examination of the facts. The case is also supportive of the review panel's power to make decisions which go to the merits of an argument in the sense of looking at the appropriateness of past decisions in the light of new evidence (in this case the cognitive limitations of people with Down's syndrome) rather than simply reviewing the processes by which those decisions were made and their conformity with policy.

Local authority complaints procedures may also be the subject of applications to the Ombudsman alleging maladministration in their operation. As applicants to the Ombudsman must normally have exhausted the local authority's complaints procedure, there is plenty of opportunity for shortcomings in those procedures to be examined. Recent findings of maladministration have included undue delay; criticism of the attendance of the local authority solicitor at review panel hearings, and failure properly to investigate complaints concerning senior officers of the authority. The Social Services Inspectorate's Third Inspection of complaints procedures in six local authorities in 1996, paid particular attention to an examination of the accessibility of the procedures to a wide range of service users, and to the linking of

complaints procedures to management systems. A number
of difficulties were uncovered.

One difficulty was the shortage of continuing training
for staff coupled with patchy information for service users
on what services were available, and how to complain.
Equal opportunities issues also needed to be addressed:

> *'social services departments should be able to
> demonstrate that the arrangements made to provide
> information about the complaints procedure in
> languages other than English and in forms which
> meet the range of special needs of service users are
> based on sound information about local populations
> and consultation with representatives of local
> community groups and organisations'*
>
> *(para. 1.16)*

There was also a fundamental concern about the ability of
front line staff to recognise expressions of dissatisfaction
as complaints and thus to apply the complaints procedure
appropriately at the problemsolving stage. This willingness
to identify and respond to dissatisfactions is obviously
crucial to user empowerment; the process of negotiation
which follows is also evidence of an approach based on
quality assurance as a concern for quality at each stage in
the process of service delivery. The Social Services
Inspectorate view is that informal problemsolving will
appropriately continue even when the complaint is
formalised at stage 2 and beyond.

SATISFACTION WITH PROCEDURES

Some interesting statistics were produced by the Social
Services Inspectorate (1996)as a result of their inspection,
both about the reasons for complaining and the ways in
which complaints were handled. The statistics cover both
child care and adult care. Services provided by social
workers from local offices accounted for 36 per cent of all
complaints; 30 per cent of complaints derived from
residential care; 15 per cent concerned day care for adults;
5 per cent concerned day care for children; 5 per cent
concerned foster care and domiciliary services accounted
for 4 per cent of all complaints. The statistics of course

derive from only that proportion of the population which is aware of the existence of complaints procedures. National statistics show a complaint rate of 5.5 per 10,000 population. Difficulties in conforming to time scales were disclosed by the Social Services Inspectorate research; indeed one of the major findings was that insufficient dedicated time was devoted to investigations. Only 46 per cent of investigations were completed within the three month time limit. Consumer satisfaction with outcomes was low; 37 per cent were satisfied, but 52 per cent were dissatisfied

Complaints about residential care are particularly problematic; there is often a difficult line to draw between the appropriateness of invoking complaints procedures; child (or adult) protection procedures and the involvement of the inspection unit. The decision about which path to follow determines who carries out the investigation, whether an independent person is appointed, and the legal nature of the outcome of the investigation (Connolly, 1996). Protection for whistleblowers in this sort of situation and acknowledgement of 'sufficient interest' is of course crucial in ensuring that concerns are dealt with quickly and appropriately.

The impression gained from looking at the workings of local authority complaints procedures is that they are in some ways treated as marginal to the performance of social services functions. They are inadequately publicised and under-utilised and are not well integrated into management systems. They operate as quality control mechanism when things go wrong but are not identified as a quality assurance tool for use by front line staff to a sufficient extent. The hope of a national system through adherence to policy guidance and the blueprint laid down in the Complaints Procedure Directions, does not appear to have been achieved; wide variations in structure and practice appear to exist as evidenced in reports from the Ombudsman and the Social Services Inspectorate. Nevertheless, the complaints procedure is potentially a good vehicle for resolving low level problems that do not have major resource implications for the local authority (Richards, 1996). Some authorities have been willing to accept a test case strategy within the complaints procedure to deal with a number of complaints on the same issue. Administratively, the outcomes of complaints should feed back into service planning, as gaps in the provision of services and problems in their implementation are highlighted.

THE LOCAL AUTHORITY MONITORING OFFICER

The Local Authority Monitoring Officer is a person whose role and function is not often explained. Very often the job is undertaken by the Chief Executive or Chief Officer of the local authority' legal department. Section 5 of the Local Government and Housing Act 1989 requires every local authority to appoint a monitoring officer who acts as an internal scrutineer of sound and legal administrative practice. His involvement is triggered whenever any proposal, decision or omission by the authority, any of its committees, or any joint committee

> 'constitutes, has given rise to or is likely to give rise to… a contravention of any rule of law or any code of practice made or approved by or under any enactment, or any such maladministration or injustice as is mentioned in Part III of the Local Government Act 1974 (Local Commissioners)'.

The role extends over all different functions of the local authority, in its various departments. The monitoring officer will investigate the matter in question and report to the appropriate committee of the local authority which has 21 days within which to consider and respond to his report. During this time any action based upon the matter under investigation is held in abeyance. If the authority declines to act on the report, referral may be made to the District Auditor. Richards (1996) commends the process as a preliminary to making a complaint:

> 'Contacting the monitoring officer may be a useful adjunct to the complaints procedure and even if the matter is not resolved satisfactorily; then it will at least be evidence that the local authority were on notice of the existence of a problem in any subsequent judicial review proceedings.'   **(p.155)**

Default powers

In the field of public law, if a local authority fails to carry out any of its social services functions, the Secretary of State can declare the authority to be in default, issue directions to ensure that the duties specified are complied with, and enforce that direction in the High Court. Default powers exist both under the Children Act 1989 (s.84) and in the new s.7D of the Local Authority Social Services Act 1970, inserted by the National Health Service and Community Care Act 1990 s.50. The Children Act power is a new one, and was inserted during the Committee stage of the Bill without debate; the default power in respect of community care functions replaced an similar provision under the National Assistance Act 1948 s.36(1).

The same principles apply to both types of default power.

- The Secretary of State must be satisfied that the local authority have failed without reasonable excuse to comply with any of their duties (not powers) which are social service functions
- The Secretary of State may make an order declaring the authority to be in default with respect to the duty in question
- Such an order may contain directions for ensuring that the duty is complied with within such period as may be specified within the order.
- Any such direction shall, on application of the Secretary of State, be enforceable by mandamus (that is by the process of judicial review in the Divisional Court).

USE OF THE DEFAULT POWER

The process is a discretionary one, and there is no recorded instance of the power having been used: nor are records kept of the number of applications made for the power to be used. The power is available only in respect of social services duties, not powers, and there is no scope for delegating the performance of these duties to any other body. Since the power has never been used, then presumably the threshold of 'manifest failure' (*R. v. DHSS and Others, ex parte Bruce* (1986) The Times, February, 8,

1986) has never been passed. The Public Law Project (1994) consider the default powers to be relevant where a local authority

- Unreasonably refuses to make an assessment
- Fails to provide statutory services when they have the resources to do so
- Fails to establish a complaints procedure
- Completely ignores a direction

Though the existence of the default power may be a barrier to a private law remedy (as in *Wyatt v. Hillingdon London Borough Council* (1978))76 L.G.R. 727) its real meaning exists at a political level. If intransigent local authorities were in conflict with the Secretary of State, the default power could be used to assert the authority of the latter. As the dispute is more likely to be about a shortage of resources provided by central government to local government, then the Secretary of State would hardly be likely to draw attention to this by use of the default procedure. The converse situation of profligate local authorities would nowadays be dealt with by 'rate capping' if not by the imposition of liability on individual councillors through the intervention of the District Auditor.

CORRESPONDENCE WITH THE DEPARTMENT OF HEALTH

People who write in to the Department of Health with a complaint about local authority services will not necessarily receive the ministerial response for which they are looking. LASSL(96)12 (Correspondence on Social Services Matters) describes the revised protocol which the Department of Health will be following in dealing with correspondence about social services matters addressed to ministers of the department by MPs, corporate bodies or members of the public. Letters containing a request for services or allegations that particular cases have been wrongly handled will usually be referred back to the local authority. The Department will only become involved where the representation relates to government policy or the case involves a breach of statutory duty. Correspondents who are dissatisfied with the outcome of a statutory complaint will be given information about the role of the local government Ombudsman.

The local government ombudsman

The Commissioner for Local Administration (or Ombudsman) may investigate allegations of injustice caused by maladministration in the performance of its functions by a local authority. The system has been in existence since 1974 and in the early days members of the public had to channel their complaints through a local councillor; though this still may be desirable, it is no longer required. There are three Regional Commissioners for England based in London, Coventry and York and one each for Wales and Scotland. The Ombudsman can :

- Investigate complaints of injustice suffered as a result of maladministration
- Look at the use of complaints procedures
- Recommend the award of compensation by the local authority.

CRITERIA FOR COMPLAINTS

The idea of an Ombudsman as an independent authority overseeing standards of public administration originated in Scandinavia. The Ombudsman cannot investigate the merits of decisions taken without maladministration (for that the complaints procedure should be used). The classic formulation of maladministration is the so-called Crossman catalogue of

'bias, neglect, inattention, delay, incompetence, ineptitude, and arbitrariness'.

No doubt there are others, but this seems a reasonable list of administrative vices in itself. Complaints must be made within twelve months (contrast three months for judicial review), and alternative rights and remedies must usually have been exhausted unless the Commissioner feels that it is not reasonable to expect the complainant to use those rights. In practice, the Ombudsman will usually investigate provided the complainant has not actually started court proceedings (Richards, 1996). An attempt is usually made to achieve a settlement without a formal investigation, and in fact only about 2.5 per cent of all complaints actually result in a final report; payments towards legal costs will be considered in exceptional cases, but the approach is investigative, not based upon a formal hearing. Complaints about social service functions are small in number – about 5 per cent of the total – but probably most effective where there is a cluster of problems about difficulty in obtaining a particular service, or where the complaint is about unfairness in the operation of local authorities' own complaints procedures. The Ombudsman service has the advantage of being free of charge, and can result in a recommendation for the payment of compensation by the local authority. The Ombudsman also has access to all relevant files and other records, and has the same powers as the High Court to compel the production of documents or the attendance of witnesses. Copies of the Ombudsman's report are public documents; a copy of the final report will be sent to all parties, and if the local authority does not act upon his recommendations the Ombudsman may publish a further report leading to a statement in an agreed form which must be published in the local press. Copies of all the local Ombudsman's reports in England can be obtained from the London address which is **21 Queen Anne's Gate, London SW1H 9BU**; they make fascinating reading for their astuteness and willingness to get to the heart of the matter in dispute.

DECISIONS OF THE OMBUDSMAN

The Ombudsman has been stringent in his criticism of local authorities for failure to implement good practice. Investigation No. 92/C/1042 into a complaint against Cleveland County Council led to a recommendation for a review of care planning procedures following the death of a resident with learning difficulties in one of the authority's homes. Maladministration was found to exist in the failure to implement a proper care programme for that resident taking into account the level of supervision required, and including her family in the process. The report is an interesting one for the stringency with which it required issues of risk assessment and risk management to be addressed. Support for the Children Act principles of partnership with parents and interagency cooperation was shown in an investigation (Complaint No. 94/A/1047 against the London Borough of Haringey) into allegations by a parent of sexual abuse against her learning disabled son. Maladministration was found in the failure of the local authority to conduct a proper child protection investigation, to involve and communicate properly with the family, and to draw up a planned strategy for the child with timescales for future action. Furthermore, there was inadequate supervision of the officers involved. All of these matters were held to constitute maladministration. Compensation of £1,000 was recommended for the injustice thus caused; plus the provision of further therapy if required. The Ombudsman also maintained a watching brief on the operation of the authority's complaints procedure by asking the authority to report back in three months time on the outcome.

Reports from the Ombudsman are sometimes used to review social services procedures or matters of policy, assessment and resource allocation. Commonplace situations, such as an inability to meet home care commitments because of staff shortages have been reviewed by the Ombudsman who has been critical of the absence of an effective policy in such cases. One such example was the investigation into Complaint No. 93/A/4250 against Westminster City Council. It is clear from the reading of the final report that difficulties arose in the context of the transfer from a direct referral system to the Domiciliary Care Service, to referral through the Council's Assessment and Care Management Service; a change that most local authorities have experienced through the introduction of the purchaser/provider split. The assumption that visits for shopping and medication and hospital discharge cases take priority over domestic cleaning is also widespread. The complainant in this case was disabled and thus entitled to a comprehensive assessment of his needs under the Disabled Persons (Services, Consultation and Representation) Act 1986; Council policy not to provide this was thus maladministration. (This entitlement to a comprehensive assessment was the same conclusion reached in the Rixon case, see p.3). Logically, as pointed out in the final report, the extent of the injustice suffered by the complainant cannot be quantified **without** such a comprehensive assessment. The lack of priority given to a cleaning service was not a matter of policy as such(though it possibly should have been) but it did fail to take into account medical need and therefore was maladministration. Failure to provide a regular cleaning service in times of staff shortage was also seen to be maladministration; this may be contrasted with the decision within the Court of Appeal in the *Gloucestershire* case that such a situation would not in itself be illegal. Practical difficulties and the need to ration scarce resources are therefore no defence to a finding not necessarily of illegality but of maladministration.

There are many examples in the Ombudsman's reports of delay in assessment and in the provision of resources; the provision of aids and adaptations by the local authority's occupational therapy service has often been highlighted. As with home care, the development of informal, or even formal, priorities to deal with very high demand has not necessarily protected the local authority from criticism. The emphasis again has been on the importance of individualised needs-led assessment where positions on waiting lists are capable of frequent revision. As a baseline, it appears that a waiting time of no more than six weeks for a first assessment is acceptable.

Recent reports of the Ombudsman have shown an awareness of complaints which cluster around eligibility criteria. Although it has been said that the Ombudsman cannot directly challenge local authority policy decisions, this too may be changing in cases where blanket policies do not take account of individual needs. This is particularly so where new care management arrangements or changes in responsibility between agencies affect long-standing service provision decisions. Such a case was an investigation into a complaint against the London Borough Council of Brent (No. 93/A/0523) concerning the ending of funding for psychotherapy by the local authority. The Ombudsman did not decide that the local authority was not entitled to stop or reduce the funding, but that it has an obligation properly to review the situation and assess the continued value and benefit of the therapy as well as its overspent budget. Furthermore, it was for the local authority itself to approach the health authority about possible alternative assistance or funding, not simply to define needs as health care needs rather than social care needs. The lack of an allocated social worker was seen as compounding the difficulties in this case. £1250 in compensation was awarded.

Actions for breach of statutory duty and negligence

The powers and duties of local authorities are the creation of statute; examples are the Children Act 1989, the Mental Health Act 1983 and the Chronically Sick and Disabled Persons Act 1970. Legislation is the means by which government consciously seeks to determine what sort of services should be provided (but not usually how much of each service); by whom and following what sort of assessment and decision-making processes. Legislation from central government sets the template within which local government operates. Unfortunately much can be lost in the translation and, unfortunately also, the courts, in deciding whether or not breaches of statutory duty have taken place in individual cases, have tended to take a noncentralist approach. The premise has been that Parliament intended to delegate the finer points of decision-making to local authorities who would then be free to take local circumstances into account, irrespective of the geographical variations in practice that this would create. Given the presumption in favour of delegation with a free hand., the courts have been reluctant to intervene, particularly where policy issues are concerned.

THE NATURE OF PRIVATE LAW ACTIONS

Actions for breach of statutory duty and actions in negligence are private law matters where compensation by way of damages is sought by individuals. They can be contrasted with judicial review where the public interest is paramount. Given that many pieces of statute law in the welfare field appear to impose explicit duties upon local authorities to provide services to people in need of support for themselves and their families, or in need of housing, or special education, then enforcement of such duties by an 'action for breach of statutory duty' might be thought commonly to be available. This is not in fact the case. There are many barriers to be overcome within an action for breach of statutory duty. There are also only a few examples of public duties which have been accepted as creating rights for individuals, enforceable through an action in negligence at common law. Nevertheless, a successful action for breach of statutory duty, or negligence at common law, is the only effective means that an individual has of obtaining significant compensation for a wrong done by the local authority.

● An action for breach of statutory duty will exist only if the statute can be construed as intending to give rise to an individual right of action.
● An action in the tort of negligence against the local authority is possible only if there is a breach of a common law duty of care.
● An individual employee of the local authority may in some cases be liable in negligence for their actions. The authority will then be liable as employer under ordinary principles of vicarious liability.

UNENFORCEABILITY OF TARGET DUTIES

Most public law duties are seen as 'target duties'; this means that they are an achievement to which local authorities are expected (by central government) to aspire. Such duties are also collectivist insofar as they exist for the benefit of the population as a whole, or a specified group within it, rather than for the benefit of individuals within that group. The distinction can be seen very clearly in the wording of s.17 of the Children Act 1989 compared to its predecessor, s.1 of the Child Care Act 1980. Section 1 of the Child Care Act 1980 read:

'It shall be the duty of every local authority to promote the welfare of children by diminishing the need to receive children into care... by providing help in kind, or exceptionally in cash.'

Section 1 had been interpreted in earlier case law as giving rise to an action for breach of statutory duty in respect of families with children in need who had been refused housing on the grounds that they were intentionally homeless. It was to avoid this sort of interpretation that s.17 of the Children Act 1989 was carefully drafted not to refer to individual circumstances but instead to say that it shall be the general duty of the local authority to safeguard and promote the welfare of children in its area who appear to be in need. A target duty of this sort is enforceable (if at all) not by an action for breach of statutory duty, but by recourse to the default powers of the Secretary of State. However, the law is developing rapidly and judicial review (the public law equivalent of a private law action for breach of statutory duty) has increasingly been used to reinterpret the duties of Social Services Departments so as to include responsibilities for children in need whose families are homeless and who themselves are therefore vulnerable to the need to be accommodated by the local authority. Obtaining a successful outcome may therefore be a matter of choosing the appropriate remedy.

The specific duties in Schedule 2 of the Children Act 1989 such as the duty to provide day care for children in need under the age of 5 and the duty to provide family centres which are an important part of the scheme of preventative work with children and families, are probably no more enforceable than the general duty in s.17. Such duties are not absolute requirements but expressed in terms of the local authority 'taking reasonable steps' or providing such services 'as they consider appropriate'. The discretion is subjectively worded. There are only two absolute duties:

1. The duty to publish information about services provided and
2. The duty to open and maintain a register of disabled people.

The great weakness of the Children Act 1989 lies in the failure properly to resource Part III provision, given its success in reinforcing preventative work as 'statutory work'. There is no mechanism within Part III itself to compel a local authority to provide services; the type and quantity of provision therefore will vary very much from one authority to another.

LIABILITY FOR DECISIONS IN CHILD CARE CASES

A recent attempt to bring an action for breach of statutory duty against a local authority under the Children Act 1989 was made in the case of *X v. Bedfordshire County Council* [1995] 3 W.L.R. 152. The House of Lords, as the highest judicial authority, took the opportunity on that occasion of hearing several cases together which concerned the liability of the local authority, and individuals employed or engaged by it, in cases involving both child protection and the assessment of special educational needs. The action against Bedfordshire County Council involved an allegation that complaints of abuse made over a number of years and concerning children within a particular family were not conscientiously followed up. A case involving Newham London Borough Council heard at the same time concerned a disputed diagnosis of sexual abuse made by a consultant psychiatrist acting within child protection procedures. The education cases against a number of local authorities involved failure to recognise and make provision for special educational needs under the Education Act 1981 (as it then was). The issues raised by these cases involved not only breach of statutory duty but also actions for breach of a common law duty of care (that is, an action in negligence for decisions involving foreseeable damage to a particular child).

What this means is that as well as the local authority having a statutory duty properly to act in the public interest and in that of individuals directly affected by its actions, or inactions, it is also arguable that alongside that duty there may exist a duty at common law owed by the authority itself or by employees of the authority not to act beyond their statutory remit in a manner which would cause harm to individuals affected by their actions. If these individual employees were liable for a breach of this common law duty then the authority would be vicariously liable for their actions, according to ordinary principles of law. Accordingly, the same facts might give rise both to an action for breach of statutory duty and to an action in negligence in common law. The judgement of the House of Lords in these cases may be seen as fundamental in setting the boundaries of administrative and professional accountability. In the event, the judgement distinguished between accountability for child protection and for educational decisions.

The House of Lords reiterated what was already known; that the existence of a private law remedy by means of a claim for breach of statutory duty was a matter of statutory construction; did Parliament intend in this particular piece of legislation that it should be enforceable on the initiative of particular individuals? In the case of a statute such as the Children Act 1989, which was concerned with child protection, no such intention was found. Nor did the local authority owe any duty of care at common law for the negligent performance of its duties. As for the duties of individual social workers; their duty was to advise the local authority on the proper course of action to take within a child protection system; they did not owe a duty to the individual child; nor did other professionals who were so retained. It was otherwise, however, in the case of education professionals. Though no action could be brought against the authority itself, for breach of statutory duty; professionals within that system such as educational psychologists, specialist advisers and head teachers did owe a duty of care to those affected by their actions as they held themselves out as possessing specialist skills in educational assessment. The authority would as employer be vicariously liable for their actions. An authority which had set up a specialist psychological service was also itself liable in negligence at common law for operational decisions made by that service.

POLICY ISSUES

Interesting questions of policy are raised. Child protection procedures (provided they conform to the rules of natural justice) have had ascribed to them a special status, verging on inviolability. As we have seen, local authority complaints procedures under the Children Act 1989 specifically do not include matters arising under Parts IV and V of the Act, relating to child protection. Now it has been recognised that an aggrieved individual may not bring a private law action against either an over-zealous or tardy authority. In addition, the immunity extends to other professionals involved in the child protection process. The policy decision was made explicit by the House of Lords; they would protect discretionary decisions within a statutory scheme lest making such decisions actionable would lead to defensive practice. On this reasoning, individual professionals as well as the authority itself needed protection in their collegiate decision making. The decision confirms Thoburn's (1986) observation that

'when things go wrong, people tend to look to procedures rather than practice for an explanation.'
By contrast, education professionals were equated with members of the medical profession who have always been

held to be individually liable for the negligent performance of their duties. Both are seen as holding themselves out to the public as possessors of special skills. The Education Authority would not be liable in its own right, except as employer. Here the reasoning follows a familiar pattern. The existence of an alternative remedy for those aggrieved with a statutory scheme has commonly been interpreted by the courts as showing Parliament's intention that the matter should be dealt with otherwise than as a breach of statutory duty. Thus the system of internal reviews (and now appeals to the Special Educational Needs Tribunal) was seen as militating against an individual right of action under the Education Act against the education authority itself except where operational decisions of the psychological service set up by it were themselves negligent. The different conclusions reached by the House of Lords under the Children Act and the Education Act respectively are a good illustration of how specific reasoning around the interpretation of a particular statute can be. So, what about other important pieces of legislation such as the Mental Health Act 1983, the National Health Service and Community Care Act 1990, or the Chronically Sick and Disabled Persons Act 1970. Can they support an individual action for breach of statutory duty, or for negligence?

INTERPRETATION OF THE MENTAL HEALTH ACT 1983

The Mental Health Act 1983 is a prime example of what may be called therapeutic law insofar as it is highly dependent upon professional judgement which focuses on the enhancement of welfare as its outcome. The terminology used is not closely construed; 'mental illness' for example is nowhere defined in the Mental Health Act 1983 but is a matter for professional interpretation. The duties that the Act imposes and the rights that it gives are largely procedural: the duty of an approved social worker properly to assess the patient; the duty if no satisfactory alternative exists to apply for admission; and the right to appeal to a mental health review tribunal . There is one duty in the Mental Health Act 1983 however which has been held to give rise for an action for breach of statutory duty and that is s.117. Section 117(2) states:

> *'It shall be the duty of the District Health Authority and the local social services authority to provide in co-operation with relevant statutory agencies, aftercare services for any person to whom this section applies until such time as the district health authority are satisfied that the person concerned is no longer in need of such services.'*

Section 117 does not define the type or quality of aftercare services to be provided, and their duration is left to the separate discretions of the health authority and the social services authority. Nevertheless in *R. v. Ealing District Health Authority ex parte Fox* [1993] 1 W.L.R. 373 the patient was in the fortunate position of having his appropriate aftercare arrangements spelled out for him. The mental health review tribunal which discharged him had used its power under s.73 of the Mental Health Act 1983 to defer discharge until a Responsible Medical Officer had been appointed to provide outpatient care. The health authority, because it disagreed with the decision of the tribunal, did not appoint a Responsible Medical Officer as directed. The patient then brought an action for judicial review seeking an order of certiorari and a declaration that the authority had erred in law in not attempting 'with all reasonable expedition and diligence' to make arrangements to enable the applicant to comply with the conditions laid down by the mental health review tribunal. Though this action was in public law, Orton J. in the course of his judgement referred to the 'continuing duty to the patient' to provide aftercare services and granted a declaration that the authority was in breach of its statutory duty under s.117 of the Mental Health Act 1983 in failing to provide aftercare services for a patient detained under s.3. This opens the door to actions for breach of statutory duty being brought in private law; most litigants however, unlike Mr Fox, will face the difficulty of quantifying the service to be provided, hence the importance here also of pressing for a written and detailed discharge plan.

SECTION 2 CHRONICALLY SICK AND DISABLED PERSONS ACT 1970

The enforceability of the service provision decision under s.2 of the Chronically Sick and Disabled Persons Act 1970 has caused some difficulty. An early decision under the Act,

Wyatt v. Hillingdon London Borough Council (1978) 76
L.G.R. 727 held that the existence of an alternative remedy
in the default powers of the Secretary of State of itself
would preclude a private claim for damages. However, the
recent decision of the House of Lords in the Bedfordshire
case (above) indicated that the mere existence of some
other statutory remedy is not necessarily decisive against
the existence of a right of action for a breach of statutory
duty. The matter in dispute in the Wyatt case was the
number of home help hours allocated to Mrs Wyatt's
personal care which she claimed were insufficient for her
needs. The situation once the service provision decision
has been made in the applicant's favour is however
different. It was common ground in the House of Lords in
the Gloucestershire case that s.2 of the Act – the duty to
make arrangements – is a duty owed to the disabled
person individually. This is so even though the **content** of
that duty may be determined by reference to the resources
of the local authority.

NATIONAL HEALTH SERVICE AND COMMUNITY CARE ACT 1990

As for the National Health Service and Community Care
Act 1990, there is nothing on the face of the Act itself to
show that it was intended to create a right of action to
those aggrieved by the nonprovision of services. In fact the
reverse is probably the case, as s.47 of the Act itself
involves only a duty to assess; entitlement to community
care services depends upon the interpretation of the
statutes listed as providing such services in s.46. A failure
to assess, or a flawed decision-making process would be
dealt with by means of judicial review. But what if the
decision were taken that a community care service such as
residential care or home care should be provided and the
local authority failed to give effect to it, for example
because a provider was no longer able to deliver the
service? In such a case, the decision having been made to
provide a service makes all the difference; the individual is
then enabled to sue for breach of statutory duty if the
service is not given. It might be thought that the obligation
to provide a service was a contractual one if this was
written into the care plan. However, a care plan is not a

contract (see p.18), but it is of evidential value in showing the local authority's intention. The Laming letter of 1992 which provided guidance on the implementation of the Act assumed that there could be such liability once a policy decision had become operationalised.

> 'once the authority has indicated that a service should be provided to meet an individual's needs and the authority is under a legal obligation to provide it or arrange for its provision the service must be provided.' **(para. 13)**

Housing authorities acting under the homelessness legislation have had to face similar claims in private law for failing to implement their own decisions within a reasonable period of time. In *R. v. Lambeth London Borough Council, ex parte Barnes (Olive)* (1993) 25 H.L.R. 140 the applicant who spent over a year waiting for suitable accommodation after being accepted as homeless was held to be entitled to damages for breach of statutory duty. This support for legal rights following a successful conclusion to the decision-making process for the applicant may be contrasted with the general reluctance of the courts to interfere with the local authority's discretionary decision as to whether or not an individual satisfies the criteria of 'homeless' or 'not intentionally homeless', under the Housing Acts.

ACTIONS IN NEGLIGENCE AGAINST INDIVIDUALS

It is well established that medical professionals will be liable in negligence towards their patients if loss is suffered as a result of their actions. The test is whether a 'responsible body of medical opinion' would have supported the action undertaken. Liability under the Mental Health Act 1983 is personal to the ASW, but he or she is protected from criminal or civil liability by s.139 unless the act was done in bad faith or without reasonable care: civil proceedings in such cases require the leave of the High Court. We have seen, following the *Bedfordshire* case, that there will be no liability for social workers and other professionals acting under child protection procedures. However, in the later case of *Barnett v. Enfield London Borough Council*, The Times, April, 22, 1997, the Court of Appeal was prepared to countenance limited liability for negligent acts on the part of social workers (and thus vicarious liability by their employers) with regard to the making of decisions with respect to children already in care. In this case the plaintiff was claiming damages for harm suffered as a result of his experiences in care through many changes of placement. Immunity from liability was said to extend in relation to *'the making of those decisions as to the future of a child which were normally made by a parent'* (which would include placement decisions); this was stated explicitly to be in recognition of the 'difficult and delicate balancing of conflicting interests' of the child, parents, foster carers and others which could be involved. However, the Court of Appeal **did** admit that Social Workers could be 'negligent in an operational manner' and therefore liable if they failed to implement decisions made (e.g. by a review meeting) or, more broadly, for failing properly to gather information upon which those decisions were made. The implication of this is that in appropriate cases assessments of the child in care could attract liability.

PROCEDURE

Though bringing an action for damages may appear attractive as a means of enforcing local authority duties, the process is likely to be a protracted one unless an early settlement is reached. Such a settlement would normally provide ex gratia compensation without admission of liability (and thus the danger of setting a precedent). If pushed to trial the process may take up to five years (according to the Public Law Project,1994). Judicial review of the disputed decision within which damages may be awarded may be a preferred alternative, though an award of damages may be limited to services which the local authority has a duty to provide rather than a discretion to provide (Richards, 1996). Also, an action for damages on its own is unlikely to provide any interim relief, whereas injunctive relief may be available in judicial review proceedings in order to maintain services until the dispute is resolved. It should also be remembered that an adverse finding from the Ombudsman may attract compensation for the complainant, though the figure will not be substantial.

Judicial review

An application for judicial review is the primary legal means for enforcing public law duties. It operates to hold public bodies to account, not on the merits of the decisions that they make, but for aspects of legality and due process in decision making. It is not an appeal process insofar as the court does not substitute its own view for that of the authority concerned, but it is a means of obtaining an authoritative declaration of the law, or a direction to the authority to 'think again'.

- Judicial review is a remedy in public law
- Is located within the Divisional Court of Queen's Bench in London
- Is usually dependent upon other remedies having been exhausted
- Is complex and will certainly be dependent upon professional legal advice.

APPROPRIATENESS OF JUDICIAL REVIEW

Applications for judicial review are not something to be embarked upon lightly. The procedure is complex and expensive. Application is to the Divisional Court of the Queen's Bench (a branch of the High Court), and leave has first to be sought. The threat of legal action may of itself be sufficient to make the local authority change its mind so as to avoid a legal precedent being set. Both the Children Act 1989 and the National Health Service and Community Care Act 1990 offer considerable scope for judicial review as each relies heavily upon the exercise of professional discretion within a broad framework of powers and duties. Usually, all alternative avenues of complaint must be exhausted before proceeding to judicial review. However, as will be seen, a judicial review may be the only appropriate forum to deal with complex legal issues and the Divisional Court itself has increasingly recognised that other means of redress are, for some issues, inappropriate. In any event, time is of the essence insofar as proceedings have to be brought promptly; normally within three months of the cause of action arising, though when the complaint is one of a continuing breach of a statutory duty (as many are) time limits are unimportant. Negotiations may have to take place with the local authority either to adjourn a application for judicial review whilst other remedies are being pursued, or to obtain a guarantee that an out of time argument will not be taken.

A person seeking judicial review must have sufficient interest in the subject matter of the case, though 'public interest' challenges have increasingly been allowed where the decision to be challenged affects an identifiable class of people. The Child Poverty Action Group and RADAR have brought cases in this way, and may also provide financial support to individuals who are willing to bring test cases to clarify points of law of general importance. Public interest groups are not themselves eligible for legal aid. Liability for costs may be a deterrent though in public interest cases a protected costs order could be granted. Whether or not an application for judicial review is pursued to its conclusion, considerable publicity may be gained by starting an action, and where an argument is based upon 'what Parliament intended' socioeconomic statistics can be used to illustrate the effect on public health or well-being of individual decisions particularly in the field of welfare benefits or employment practices. Thus an application for judicial review may be used as a campaigning tool as well as a strictly legal remedy.

SCOPE OF JUDICIAL REVIEW

It is only 'public' bodies, for example; local authorities, health authorities, government departments and prison boards of visitors whose actions are amenable to judicial review. This is because they act under statutory powers. Increasing use is being made of judicial review as a remedy, and there are a number of reasons for this. One reason lies in the nature of some modern day legislation which may have had a swift passage through Parliament with few opportunities for close scrutiny. Such legislation may additionally be drafted in the broadest of terms with few details as to its implementation written in. The National Health Service and Community Care Act 1990 is a good example of this; Part 3 of the Act, which introduces fundamental changes to the system of assessing need and making provisions for community care services is contained in only nine sections of the Act and provides no detail on how such an assessment is to be carried out, or how resources are to be allocated. This means that the implementation of the Act is left to be explained in policy and practice guidance; the legal status of which is only just being clarified. The courts are able to challenge such framework legislation without challenging the sovereignty of Parliament.

CONCERN WITH PROCESS

Judicial review respects also the integrity of decision makers by being concerned not with the merits of the decision, but with the process by which the decision is reached. The decision may be

1. Ultra vires: that is, outside the statutory powers of the body making the decision. Alternatively, there may be a failure properly to exercise a power or a duty given by statute.
2. Based on a misinterpretation of the law
3. Unreasonable or irrational
4. Procedurally incorrect or unfair.

The central principle of judicial review is the principle of legality; that the decision maker must understand correctly the law that regulates his decision-making power and must give effect to it. Thus in *Brunyate v Inner London Education Authority* [1989] 1 W.L.R. 542, the Inner London Education Authority's removal of school governors for their failure to support ILEA's educational policy was held to be unlawful as usurping the governors' independent function under the Education Act. Within the broad head of 'illegality' there exists also the irrelevancy principle; a decision is only within statutory powers if it takes all relevant information into account, but does not take irrelevant information into account. So in *R. v. Lewisham London Borough Council, ex parte Shell UK Ltd.* [1988] 1 All E.R. 938, a boycott of Shell products because of their South African connection was held not to be lawful because of irrelevant considerations or motives.

Even if a decision is within the 'four corners' of the

powers granted to a local authority, it may be nevertheless be considered to be so irrational or unreasonable that no reasonable authority could have reached that conclusion. This is often referred to as 'Wednesbury unreasonableness' after the famous judgement of Lord Greene MR in the case of *Associated Provincial Picture Houses Ltd v. Wednesbury Corporation* [1948] 1 K.B. 223, where the point at issue was the local authority's exercise of its discretion to allow cinemas to open on Sundays. There are a number of examples where this power has been used where an authority was clearly in conflict with central government. An outstanding example is *Backhouse v. Lambeth London Borough Council* (1972) 116 S.J. 802 where the local authority had increased rents from £7 to £18,000 so as to seek to avoid fair rents legislation with which it disagreed.

Procedural impropriety includes failure to establish proper procedures, failure to follow procedures once they are set up, and failure to give a fair hearing when rights are at stake. Procedural impropriety is a basis for judicial review in cases where the decision itself is legally correct. The principle which is invoked is that of 'natural justice'. On a modern day interpretation, natural justice is wide enough to cover many aspects of maladministration which in another context would attract the attention of the Ombudsman. It includes the rule against bias (*nemo judex in causa sua*); the right to a fair hearing (*audi alteram partem*); the doctrine of legitimate expectation and the duty to give reasons. The rule against bias operates so as to prevent interested parties from being involved in decision making, or to prevent the prejudgement of an issue by parties who have already been exposed to an opinion on the outcome of the case. The right to a fair hearing differs in its content according to the circumstances of the case and the nature of the inquiry. In *R. v. Avon County Council ex parte Crabtree* [1996] 1 F.L.R. 502 it did not prevent executive members of an adoption panel hearing a recommendation for deregistration in which they had previously been involved; adoption panels are not expected to function as judicial bodies, and it is expected that members of administrative bodies may well have some prior knowledge of the case. At a minimum a fair hearing involves the giving of notice, some detail of the opposing case, and a reasonable opportunity to present one's own case. The doctrine of legitimate expectation is particularly appropriate in situations where public bodies have promulgated their own eligibility criteria, or have developed 'past practice' on procedural issues, Finally, a duty to give reasons, may be seen as a prerequisite for any informed challenges to decision-making whether through the courts or otherwise.

REMEDIES IN JUDICIAL REVIEW

An action for judicial review can normally only be brought when all other remedies have been exhausted. There are however exceptions to this: where for instance an obvious point of law is involved; where it is important for the matter to be resolved quickly; or where a general policy or matter of principle is to be challenged. One advantage of judicial review is that an injunction may be granted to compel a local authority to provide a service, or alternatively to refrain from a certain course of action, pending a full hearing. No other remedy offers the opportunity for such interim relief. On final hearing the court has the power to award the following remedies:

- An order of certiorari to quash an invalid decision and to enable the authority to think again (though without any guarantee that the same decision will not be made)
- An order of prohibition to prevent an illegal or improper course of action from being taken
- An order of mandamus to enforce the performance of a statutory duty
- A declaration about the law or the rights of the individual (the *Gillick* case on 'competent' minors was decided in this way)
- An injunction to prevent a breach of the law or, as a mandatory injunction, to enforce the performance of a statutory duty
- Compensation by way of damages for breach of a private right by nonperformance of a public law duty. In this case the claim for damages must be linked to a claim for one of the other remedies.

All the above remedies are discretionary. The court need not order any remedy, even though it finds in the applicant's favour. In particular, a remedy would not be granted if it would not practically affect the decision to be taken: for example in the *Daniels* case *R. v. North West Thames Regional Health Authority & Secretary of State for Health, ex parte Daniels* [1993] 4 Med. L.R. 364, an order of certiorari was refused even though the Health Authority had been found in breach of its obligation to consult on the closure of a regional transplant unit. Since the reallocation of staff and transfer of resources had already gone ahead, any order requiring the Secretary of State for Health to think again would not have changed the final decision. This case is a good illustration of the limits of judicial review where strategic decision-making is concerned, and highlights the difference between appeal (for substituted decisions on the merits of a case) and review.

HEADS OF REVIEW

Case law in the field of child care and community care illustrate the possibilities and the limits of judicial review at all stages in the process of decision making: assessment; care planning; monitoring and review.

FAILURE TO EXERCISE A DISCRETION

When a local authority is given a discretion to act by statute, the courts expect that discretion actually to be exercised. In *R. v. Kingston London Borough Council, ex parte T* [1994] 1 F.L.R. 798 a 16 year old girl asked for the family with which she was living to be recognised as foster carers so that they could receive a fostering allowance. The local authority refused on the basis that she had no need of accommodation under s.20 of the Children Act 1989, being already well settled with the family. This was successfully challenged by way of judicial review, on the basis that she was a child in need whose welfare might call for intervention by the local authority in the future. The local authority had failed to exercise its discretion to assess her future needs.

FETTERING DISCRETION

Just as a local authority which has a discretion must exercise it, so must the local authority decide each

application on its merits. This prevents local authorities
from imposing blanket policies to which there are no
exceptions. Thus a policy which said that social services
departments would in no circumstances offer assistance to
intentionally homeless families would be unlawful. Any
strict application of eligibility criteria for community care
services would also be unlawful, if it prevented
consideration of individual circumstances.

IMPROPER DELEGATION

Many public bodies consult together before reaching a
final decision on any given case; indeed this is the essence
of multidisciplinary working which may become
institutionalised into child protection procedures or the
care programme approach applied to mental health
services. This does not mean that a collective responsibility
is created in the legal sense. The individual social services
authority or health authority remains responsible for the
final decision. Clements (1996) argues that this means that
decisions on the provision of aids and adaptations under
the Chronically Sick and Disabled Persons Act 1970 remain
with the social services authority and cannot be delegated
to housing authorities which determine the
appropriateness of structural alterations or provision of
grants. These matters are associated but not determinative.
The responsibility of the primary decision-making
authority in the provision of services has developed
quickly to impose accommodation duties on Social
Services Departments in respect of children in need and
asylum seekers in circumstances where the housing
authority had no duty to act (see p. 21). This inability of
authorities to divest themselves of responsibility for
people whose predominant needs are not central to social
services functions emphasises the marginality that these
groups are perceived to have.

The funding of services for pupils with special
educational needs was considered in the case of *R. v.
Hillingdon London Borough Council, ex parte Governing
Body of Queensmead School*, The Times, January, 9, 1997.
Here it was decided that the local authority had a
nondelegable duty to arrange that the special educational
provision specified in a statement was provided for the

child and that responsibility for this could not be delegated to the School. This meant that the local authority was required to give the school sufficient funds to fulfil the duty properly and could not require the school to subsidise the child's needs from its own resources. Potentially the same principle could apply to other statutory services such as residential care which the local authority has a duty to provide and thus a duty properly to fund. through its use of contracts.

Local authority responsibilities for and towards independent providers of service will be a key area for concern as the ramifications of the purchaser / provider split are felt, particularly in community care. What is the situation where the care provided by an independent provider is unsatisfactory? The Registered Care Homes Regulations 1984 (reg. 17) requires homes to have their own complaints procedures of which individual residents should be informed in writing. However, those who do not wish to use this procedure may go directly to the local authority's own complaints procedure. The provider who is in breach of contractual terms will be responsible for those breaches to the local authority. The point has not yet been decided, but the local authority may itself be liable in negligence if there is a breach of a duty of care on their behalf, certainly in relation to premises and services (like residential care) which the authority itself has a duty to inspect.

LEGITIMATE EXPECTATION

The doctrine of legitimate expectation is a useful one in challenging local authority decisions. There are both procedural and substantive elements to the doctrine. The former was developed from the GCHQ case where an expectation was upheld that negotiations between government and the civil service unions should take place before major changes in working patterns were introduced. It has been used successfully to challenge local authority plans to close Part III accommodation without adequate consultation of residents in *R. v. Devon County Council, ex parte Baker and R. Durham County Council, ex parte Curtis* [1993] 91 L.G.R. 479. A decision based on adequate consultation is less likely to be challengeable for failure to take relevant matters into account (see below). Adequate consultation will include a reasonable period of notice that a decision is to be taken; informed discussion of the alternatives; and a considered approach to any representations that are made.

The substantive element of legitimate expectation is based upon reliance that local authorities will adhere to their own published policies, whether in community care plans or elsewhere. People whose personal circumstances appear to accord with published criteria but who are nevertheless refused a service may challenge the local authority on this ground.

TAKING RELEVANT MATTERS INTO ACCOUNT

'Relevant matters' to be taken into account in decision-making in community care, now clearly includes Policy Guidance from the Department of Health, as this is issued under s.7 of the Local Authority Social Services Act 1970. Para. 3 requires local authorities to involve users in the assessment process so that the resulting services take into account their preferences. Thus in *R. v. North Yorkshire County Council, ex parte Hargreaves* (1994) 30 September, EO/878/94 a failure directly to interview a person with a learning disability so as to consider her preferences for respite care was held to be a failure properly to assess; consultation with her brother as carer being an inadequate substitute.

Also in the field of learning disability, the judgement of the court in the Mark Hazell case (see above) explored differing interpretations of the word 'need' and concluded that psychological needs should be taken into account as well as physical needs when undertaking a comprehensive assessment. The proper interpretation of 'need' was of course the point at issue in the *Gloucestershire* line of cases; particularly, the extent to which resources could be taken into account in assessing need as well as in the provision of services to meet that need. The House of Lords judgement supporting the local authority's interpretation of need as including resources was a victory for distributive rather than individual justice, In effect it upheld the legality of local authority eligibility criteria which are pitched at the level at which resources can support a given demand for services. The judgement does not however mean that extraordinary personal circumstances should not be considered, nor that a local authority will not be held to be acting unreasonably if it pitches the criteria too high.

PROCEDURAL IMPROPRIETY

If a local authority has laid down a particular procedure for its operational staff to follow, then it is expected that such a procedure will be followed. This expectation would apply to child protection procedures, as formalised by the Area Child Protection Committee. The *Devon* case (*R. v. Devon County Council ex parte L*, Journal of Child Law April/June 1991 pp. 86 - 88) in which procedures were not used, has rightly been criticised as being out of line with this general principle. In that case, families who had become involved with a man suspected by social workers of child sexual abuse, were told that their children were in jeopardy unless he left the household; with the result that a number of his relationships collapsed. The man applied for an injunction to restrain the local authority from similar courses of action in relation to him in the future. No prosecution had been brought against this man, and child protection procedures were not used to obtain his view of the situation, or to assess the risks to any child. Nevertheless the injunction was refused.

If the matter had gone to case conference then procedural safeguards for individuals involved in the process would have been upheld by judicial review. In particular, he would have been entitled to be told the case against him and to make representations to the conference (although no right of attendance has yet been confirmed). In *R. v. Norfolk County Council v. M* [1989] Q.B. 619, the applicant was held to be entitled to be informed in advance of a decision to place his name as a suspected abuser on the child protection register, given the serious nature of this decision which affected his continued employment. There is no clear right to be granted legal representation. However, in a case dealing with prison discipline, *R. v. Home Secretary, ex parte Tarrant* [1985] Q.B. 251, Webster J. commented that there could well be situations where having regard to the seriousness or the complexity of the charges, no authority properly directing itself could reasonably decide not to allow legal representation. Gordon, (1995), discusses this and other cases which support the presumption that a friend or supporter should be allowed to be present at a hearing to give advice and take notes (appropriately of course, given the nature of the inquiry). Knowing how to present one's case in the sense of what evidence the decision-making body is looking for may be crucial; and is thus a part of natural justice; *R. v. Mental Health Review Tribunal, ex parte Clatworthy* [1985] 3 All E.R. 699.

GIVING REASONS FOR DECISIONS

Though there is no absolute duty placed on public bodies to give reasons for their decisions, natural justice will require reasons to be given for those decisions which affect individual liberty, or where there is a departure from an accepted standard which needs explanation. So in *R. v. Mental Health Review Tribunal, ex parte Clatworthy* [1985] 3 All E.R. 699 the House of Lords held that there was a duty upon the Home Secretary to give reasons for tariff decisions in respect of mandatory life prisoners before referring their cases to the parole board. The issue was one of personal liberty and the context was a departure from the recommendation of the trial judge as to the tariff. The reasoning behind the judgement was that an informed challenge could not be made to the Home Secretary's recommendation unless the reasoning behind it was known. A failure to give reasons, or reasons which are less than 'adequate or intelligible' may lead to the inference that a decision is unlawful.

THE EUROPEAN DIMENSION

Challenges to decision-making may have a European dimension in one of two ways:

- They may allege a breach of European Community Law by a member state or
- They may allege a breach of the European Convention on Human Rights.

The status of these two types of European law is quite different; European Community Law is directly enforceable in the domestic court; but the Articles of the European Convention on Human Rights are only indirectly enforceable, as the Convention has not been adopted into English law.

Domestic law may not in some cases provide an appropriate remedy, particularly when it is national legislation itself which is impugned. In such cases there is the possibility of recourse to the European Convention on Human Rights. This is most likely in relation to Article 6 (due process in the determining of civil rights and obligations) and Article 8 (respect for family life and privacy). Complaint must be made in the first instance to the European Commission; and within six months of the exhaustion of domestic remedies. One of the best known cases in which a violation of the Convention was held to have taken place was the *Gaskin* case on access to information on social services files which led to the enactment of the Access to Personal Files Act 1987.

The European Commission which interprets the Convention prior to referral to the European Court it has found in favour of parents in a number of cases relating to contact with children in care, and was instrumental in having a right to challenge deprivation of contact written into the Children Act 1989. Criticism of the administrative process of passing parental rights resolutions in respect of children voluntarily accommodated also led to the abandonment of this route into care.

European Community Law, by contrast, is directly enforceable in the English courts by virtue of Britain's membership of the European Community. In complex cases, particular reference may be made for an interpretative judgement from the European Court. European Community Law is largely concerned with economic rights and in the *Marshall* case was used to challenge differential retirement ages for men and women which were outside the scope of the Sex Discrimination Act. Rights in social security law have also been tested against standards required by European Community Law.

Conclusion

An attempt has been made to illustrate how, at various points within the local authority decision making process, decisions can go awry and deviate not only from principles of good administration, but even from legal imperatives. In order to meet the range of such problems, a number of ways have developed to challenge local authority decisions internally (through the complaints procedure); and externally, within the political system (through the Ombudsman and use of the default powers), and within the legal system (through judicial review and actions for breach of statutory duty). The justification for such systems lies in public accountability, and, to a lesser extent, in striving for effectiveness and efficiency in the use of resources, both physical resources and human resources.

Quality in the provision of local authority services is maintained and monitored in a number of different ways: these mechanisms may variously be termed bureaucratic; professional; judicial and political (Thoburn, 1986). Bureaucratic control is designed to ensure accountability to a particular local authority's policies and procedures and is seen in the use of procedures manuals and managerial supervision. Professionalism is developed through training which integrates knowledge, skills and values, lending integrity to decision making; though it may lead to dilemmas for the practitioner working within a bureaucratic structure. Judicial oversight of decision making has a centralising tendency within which commentary upon and correction of local practice can take place. Political accountability and political action are two different things. Political accountability in a legal and organisational sense refers to the imperative of reporting actions back to the Social Services Committee of the Local Authority and also to the acceptance of the legitimacy of resource allocation decisions as being democratically determined. Political action may also be campaigning; to change systems, not to work within them: it may be less expensive and more effective than legal action, because it is not constrained by conventional ways of conceptualising problems.

Motivations as well as remedies fall into two categories; individual and collective. People may challenge particular decisions or whole classes of decisions out of a desire to change things for themselves, or out of a desire to be a 'test case' to change systems. Group problems may however be greater than the sum of the individual grievances, particularly when they are rooted in structural problems such as poverty and discrimination. Decisions also have their own particular hierarchy: some decisions (such as the making of a care order) are seen as so important that they can be dealt with only by a judicial forum; others, for example, the choice of a placement for a child in care are matters of administrative discretion. However, as recent decisions under the Children Act 1989 have shown, the courts are increasingly pushing to extend their influence into what was formerly seen as the sphere of administrative prerogative. This is contrary to the argument advanced by King & Trowell (1993) that the law is overemphasised as a truthfinding system, and that the scrutiny of professional decisions by the court is neither appropriate nor necessary whenever conflict arises between statutory agencies and the parent and child as how the child's interests are best served. For the courts, the argument is that they have been made the final custodians of the welfare of the child.

Judicial review has increasingly been used to challenge local authorities' interpretation of the law. To an extent, this is inevitable given the minimalist nature of much modern legislation. Much public attention has been focused on these cases, which have been as much a focus for campaigning, as they have been a focus for the need for legal clarity. Anyone embarking upon judicial review will need to have a strategy worked out for if they should lose, or for if they should win. Perhaps the most worrying trend in judicial review from the point of view of social services departments has been the willingness to use them as a residual welfare safety-net. This is disaster for interagency cooperation, and also for the rational allocation of agency resources. This problem is in large part the result of a welfare system which is based on needs rather than rights. The introduction of a Bill of Rights as an attribute of citizenship would necessitate these issues being debated on the political stage. A Bill of Rights would also meet a further criticism that substantive issues (how much of what type of service) have been neglected in favour of procedural remedies. Local authority complaints procedures have been in existence now for more that five years and have not produced statements of entitlement (or even examples of good practice) which have made national headlines. They have been parochial in their operation and interest in them has focused more on questions of procedure rather than substance. A major deficiency has been a failure adequately to publicise the existence of the procedures for the general public and to integrate their use into local authority processes from assessment onwards. But possibly the most effective way to open up local authority decisions to challenge is to inform people of what those decisions relate to: what sorts of services the local authority provide; to what sorts of people and in what sorts of circumstances. Age Concern (1994) and Mencap (1996) have each produced research which shows that local authorities, despite government guidance to the contrary, are very poor at telling people what they do. The right to information is in this context the basic right on which all others are predicated, and should therefore be the next focus for those who wish to challenge local authority decisions.

Table of cases

References

Age Concern (1994) *The Next Steps: Lessons for the Future of Community Care* London: Age Concern

Aldgate, J. & Simmonds, J. (eds.) (1988) *Direct Work with Children: A Guide for Social Work Practitioners* London: Batsford

Aldgate, J. & Tunstill, J. (1995) *Making Sense of Section 17: Implementing Section 17 of the Children Act – the first 18 months* London: HMSO

Braye, S. & Preston-Shoot, M. 'Partners in Community Care? Rethinking the Relationship between the Law and Social Work Practice' *Journal of Social Welfare and Family Law* 1974 pps. 163-183

Burgner Report (1996) *Regulating Social Services* London: DoH

Clements, L. (1996) *Community Care and the Law* London: LAG

Clements, L. (1997) 'Can't Pay, Must Pay' *Community Care* 13-19 February 1997 pps 28-29

Connolly, J. 'Scaling the Wall' *Community Care* 11-17 July 1996 pps 26-28

Coulshed, V. (1991) *Social Work Practice: An Introduction.* Basingstoke: Macmillan

Cragg, S. (1996) 'Community Care Update' *Legal Action* September 1996 pps. 16-18

Day, P., Klein, R. & Redmayne, S. (1996) *Why Regulate? Regulating Residential Care for Elderly People Bristol:* The Policy Press

DoH (1989) *The Children Act 1989: Policy and Practice in Regulations and Guidance* London HMSO

DoH (1990) *Community Care in the Next Decade and Beyond Policy Guidance* (1990) London DoH

DoH (1991) *Managers' Guide to the Implementation of the Act* London

DoH. (1991) *Practitioners' Guide to the Implementation of the Act* London

DoH (1992) *Committed to Quality: Quality Assurance in Social Services Departments* London: HMSO

DoH (1993) *Diversification and the Independent Residential Care Sector* London: HMSO

Giller, H. (1993) *Children in Need: Definition, Management and Monitoring* Social Information Services

Gordon, R. (1996) *Judicial Review: Law and Procedure* London: Sweet & Maxwell

Gordon, R. & Mackintosh, N. (1996) *Community Care Assessments: A Practical Legal Framework* London: FT Law & Tax

King, M. & Trowell, J. (1992) *Children's Welfare and the Law: the limits of legal intervention* London: Sage

Lynch, G. & Pope, B. (1990) *Involving Clients and Staff in the Development of a Quality Assurance System*: Social Services and Social Information Systems Manchester: Social Information Systems

Mencap (1996) *Community Care: Britain's Other Lottery* London: Mencap

Middleton, L. (1997) *The Art of Assessment* Birmingham: Venture Press

Marchant, C. 'What Comes First?' *Community Care* July 15, 1993. P.18

Public Law Project (1994) *Challenging Community Care Decisions* London: PLP

Richards, M. (1996) *Community Care for Older People: Rights, Remedies and Finances* Bristol: Jordans

Smale, G. & Tuson, G. with Biehal, N and Marsh, P. (1993) *Empowerment, Assessment, Care Management and the Skilled Worker* London : HMSO

Smith, C. *The Local Authority: Responsibility and Accountability in Child Care Planning* BAAF Selected Seminar Papers 1995/6

Social Services Inspectorate (1996) *The Inspection of Complaints Procedures in Local Authority Social Services Departments, 3rd Overview Report* London: DoH

Thoburn, J. 'Quality Control in Child Care' *Br. J. Social Work* (1986) 16, 543-556

White Paper (1997) *Social Services – Achievement and Challenge*